Kathy,

Oak Ridge

A special place - made more special by special friends.

Sweeping Out the Attic

Tales, Topics, and Small Talk from the Nooks and Crannies of a Well-Worn Mind

Thanks for being one of them!

Jerry L. Harris

Kathy,

Oak Ridge - A special time...
A special place - made more
special by special friends

Thanks for being one of them!

Love,
Dorris

Sweeping Out the Attic

Tales, Topics, and Small Talk from the Nooks and Crannies of a Well-Worn Mind

JERRY L. HARRIS

First Printing, 2018

ISBN-10: 1-938271-41-6
ISBN-13: 978-1-938271-41-0

Library of Congress Control Number: 20189498940

Two Peas Publishing
PO Box 1193
Franklin, TN 37065

www.twopeaspublishing.com

Table of Contents

Introduction

Sweeping Out the Attic documents a few of the tales, essays, and at times utter nonsense that I have written over the last few years. Most of my writings were not originally written for publication but were intended to entertain old friends and family members. Some of my friends found my writings interesting enough that they urged me to combine them into a book that my future generations could read. They claim I have the "Write Stuff" that will either prove or perhaps disprove that I was more than just a crazy old man.

Some friends good-naturedly threatened to kill me if I published this book. And one wife threatened to do the same. She is my only wife, and I hope no one calls her a widow any time soon. Other friends and acquaintances, and they were in the majority, offered me free beer for every time I do not mention their names in a story or essay. So now you know the reason for this book. Free Beer. Because of my fondness for Bud Lite and Miller High Life, many of the names have been deleted.

Most of the readings in this book are based on personal relationships and on specific places or events. The reader does not really need to know the person, place, event, context or reason I wrote about a specific subject. I believe we all have enough similar experiences in our lives that no matter where you are from or live, you may find a degree of familiarity, nostalgia, or perhaps even intimacy in some of the tales and situations unveiled herein. And in some cases, you will be challenged not to laugh out loud.

So, come. You are invited to look into the nooks and crannies of an old man's mind. You may be surprised at what you find inside. And as to the factual accuracy of what you are about to read, I neither confirm nor deny anything. You will just have to judge for yourself.

–The Author

School Days and Class Reunions

The Kiss

One of the most important lessons I ever learned during my Oak Ridge, Tennessee, school years had absolutely nothing to do with academics. But it did have to do with school... and girls...and field trips. So thank you, Oak Ridge Schools, for a lesson well learned. Neither my education nor my love life would have been complete without you. It is a long story, but I will try to be brief. And by the way, names have been changed to protect the guilty.

It happened on a Friday during the first week of May. The year was 1955. Early on that fateful day, my Robertsville Junior High School eighth grade class boarded the bus for a long-awaited field trip to Gatlinburg and the Smoky Mountains. I got on that bus as a shy, quiet, well behaved and naive student who would not have stood out even in a crowd of one. I mean, we are talking about a guy who had yet to experience his first real kiss and was only months away from becoming a high school freshman.

On the way to the mountains, the bus went through a couple of tunnels. The first tunnel was a learning experience for some of my more sophisticated and worldly classmates who had paired off with their favorite, at least for this day, members of the opposite sex. The second tunnel and the ensuing darkness that enveloped the bus caused some strange noises to emanate from the rear part of the vehicle. If I had not known better, I would swear that someone had been kissing back there. But upon emergence from the tunnel, a careful look showed that all my classmates were calmly staring toward the front and presented no reason for any chaperone to be alarmed.

Sally Ann Reynolds was one of the most popular girls in the class and the secret love of my life. And as usual, she had barely even looked at me all day. Suddenly it was late afternoon and time to get started for home. So there I was, sitting in an aisle seat beside one of my buddies when I felt a tap on my shoulder. The sweetest voice this side of heaven said, "Jerry why don't you come sit on the back row with me?" Fortunately, I maintained my cool and didn't pass out from either the excitement or trepidation. I very calmly jumped up and tore to the back of the bus and was already sitting anxiously when Sally Ann finally caught up to take her place beside me.

But the best–and maybe the worst–was yet to come.

Sally Ann whispered in my ear, "When we reach the tunnel turn your face my way and lean toward me. I have a surprise for you. We will have about three-to-four seconds and then will have to separate and look toward the front again." Well, we were about seven miles from that tunnel but, believe it or not, it took about sixteen hours (or was it days?) to get there. At least it seemed like that long to this anxious first-year teenager.

Finally, the tunnel encapsulated us. I quickly turned and leaned toward her. And it happened. I felt these most delicious and magical lips on my face and knew that I had finally arrived. I had hit the big time. My lips were virgin no longer. This was no spin-the-bottle game for kids. I was mentally counting my three seconds of bliss but must have been slow because the lips were gone at the count of two.

Just as I reached three, the bus emerged from the tunnel and there was light again. I quickly opened my eyes and immediately saw that other face just inches away from mine. But it was not Sally Ann. It was the face of big ole' Joe Wilson who had been sitting on Sally's other side. I admit that I panicked. Then I finally realized that Sally Ann was still between us but had bent over to tie her shoe.

But I came home a smarter man.

Thanks to you, Oak Ridge Schools, I learned some life-long lessons: 1) To avoid any surprises or substitutes, always put your arms around a girl when you are kissing her, especially if it is dark, and 2) it's okay to close your eyes when kissing a girl but if there is enough light, peek just to be sure you're kissing the right person.

And finally, here it is sixty-some years later, and I still don't know who I kissed. Was that fateful day in May 1955 the best or worst day of my life?

Why Attend a Class Reunion?

Does the below story sound familiar to anyone?

"I understand that the Oak Ridge, Tennessee, high school class of 1959 is having another reunion. Big deal. For those of you signed up to go, go and have your fun without me. I am not the least bit interested in attending. You never really liked me in high school. In fact, most of you never even knew me except as just another face in the crowd that lived outside the "in" circles. So why should I expect anything to be different now.

For you see, I was the girl/boy that didn't really fit in. I wasn't a jock. I belonged to no social clubs nor participated in group activities, mostly because I was never invited. I didn't dance well, but that was ok because no one ever invited me to dance anyway. And I guess I was ugly since I rarely or never had a date to any of the dances, football games, or movies that everyone else talked about. I was picked on a lot, maybe even bullied at times. Perhaps I was a loner or what we now call a geek. This was partly caused by my shyness but more so because you chose to exclude me from all your activities. Whether that was from intentional neglect or merely being insensitive to the wants and needs of others made no difference. I spent many Friday and Saturday nights at home, sometimes with a tear in my eye and sometimes with a little

Class of 1959 Reunion

bitterness in my heart. And when you do not keep in touch for years then suddenly invite me to attend an event to relive my high school experiences, I cannot take the invitation seriously, and the bitterness tries to resurface once again.

Why should I go to a class reunion now and reawaken all the frustration and heartbreak of a part of my life that I would just as soon forget? Besides, there are other issues. My body has changed over the years. I am much fatter/thinner than I was; my hair is gray or maybe gone. I don't move well anymore and have more ailments than most others my age. I have been less successful than many of my classmates and don't want to give them an opportunity to flaunt their successes in life. I guess you can say that even if my high school years had been more enjoyable, I would be embarrassed for my old classmates to even see me as I am now. So, go have your reunion. I am content to miss it and will be happier if I don't attend."

Well, let me tell you that much of this story once applied to me. I successfully avoided going to our high school reunions for almost fifty years. And my goodness, how time made a difference. I finally and begrudgingly attended our 50th-anniversary reunion. And I don't know whether I was disappointed or elated by what I found. My expectations were so different than what actually occurred that my life was positively changed for the better.

What I found was that the old cliques were gone. Those handsome guys and good-looking girls of our youth were now seventy-something years old, and many were unrecognizable without their name tags. Most had gained weight, and many had not aged gracefully. There were some there in much worse health than I, and most of them were handling it with grace and even laughter. No one was elitist or stuck-up or egotistic. Everyone I encountered was nice, friendly, and seemed genuinely glad to see me and meet my spouse. And while a few old stories during the weekend brought a sense of melancholy, most of my exchanges with old acquaintances brought nothing but enlightenment. The most important thing I found, however, is that we were all still teenagers at heart with the same hopes and dreams for the future. It just goes to confirm that birthdays are nothing more than a chronological measurement of time and in no way measure the heart of the person or the youthfulness of the mind.

The frustrations, fears, sadness, and loneliness of my high school years were not unique. I found out that those I had envied

Wildcat Den (circa 1959)

the most and categorized as the "most snobbish or elite of the in crowd" were little different than me. The uncertainties they had felt were in some ways very similar to my own. While I blamed them for my failure to become closer to others in high school, they had the same misguided opinions of me. We had misunderstood each other for fifty years, and now suddenly things had changed. More than a little understanding and even forgiveness took place.

For me personally, fifty years of real or imagined neglect became past history, and a new beginning with old classmates fostered new friendships and a deeper strengthening of old ones. The ill feelings of the past are gone. A new future awaits.

The Ties That Bind

If you think us sophisticated adults who came through the Oak Ridge, Tennessee, school system are stereotypical East Tennessee hillbillies, so be it. Read no further. This story has nothing to do with how people look, how many teeth they have, or whether the only real music in the world originated from the Bristol Sessions or the 1940s-1950s broadcasts coming out of WSM's Ryman Auditorium on Saturday nights. This story does have to do with what happened on the weekend of my last Oak Ridge High School Class of 1959 reunion. And yes, it happened in East Tennessee, but it could have happened anywhere.

They did not know each other very well in high school. They traveled in different circles, had different interests, had few mutual friends and lived on opposite ends of town. Oh, by the way, they were also the opposite sex. They went fifty-some years as barely casual acquaintances. It was not until the last reunion that they got to know each other well. And, boy, did they ever.

Both were happily married, maybe once, maybe twice; who knows? It makes no difference. Both attended the reunion without their spouses. During the evening at the old Wildcat Den on Saturday night, they somehow found each other. Over the course of the evening, they spent a lot of time just talking about the old days, mutual interests they had in common, and other mundane things just to make conversation. Nothing sexual; nothing romantic; no ulterior motives of any kind. But something profound happened. Eleven o'clock came and went; the disc jockey shut down; the reunion organizer thanked everyone for coming, and everyone started leaving.

Although it wasn't planned, He and She suddenly found themselves alone in the parking lot with each other. Everyone else had vacated the premises and returned to their motels or homes. Both felt somewhat awkward as they bid each other goodnight. And as old high school friends often do in situations like this, He leaned forward to give her a completely innocent and friendly goodnight kiss on the cheek.

Then something crazy happened.

Just as he puckered up and his lips neared her cheek, the last car leaving the parking lot backfired. Startled, she turned to see what was going on, rotating her lips to the exact spot her cheek had been just a second before. Sure enough, you know what happened. Or do you?

Yes, their lips came into contact with each other. But just then the car backfired again. Both mouths opened in reaction. The ensuing events are hard to explain, but I will do the best I can based on the sketchy details that I have.

Somehow in the instant of time that their lips met, purely accidental of course, his tongue somehow slipped between the gap in her teeth and penetrated deeply into her mouth. Shocked at what was happening, he quickly tried to withdraw his tongue. Well, somehow, the cap on her tongue stud had come loose, and as he tried to remove his tongue, he cut it fairly severely on the sharp tip of the stud.

The swelling was immediate, and the gap in the teeth was not that wide. The tongue simply would not come out. Well, they pushed and pulled and tugged and twisted, but nothing worked. The more they squirmed, the further the tongue slid into the gap and the closer their bodies were to each other. In trying to push her somewhat away, He somehow caused a couple of buttons to pop loose on her blouse. A bad situation was getting worse.

In the predicament they were in, even talking to each other was impossible. And obviously from the blouse fiasco, using hand communications were evidently making matters worse. But these were Oak Ridge High School graduates. They were smart. Their lips may have been confined, but their fingers still worked. Out comes the smartphone and 911 was successfully dialed.

After being unable to describe to the operator what the problem was, they hung up and tried again. This time they texted 911 and gave their location.

The EMT first responders were there within a few minutes. And give them credit. They did not laugh. After all, these were professionals. After thoroughly examining He and She, then doing a little more pushing and pulling and tugging and twisting of their bodies, one of the EMTs demonstrated his exceptional skills by applying a previously undocumented medical technique that immediately remedied the situation. The EMT wiggled his left index finger into the corner of her lower mouth while using his right index finger to lift her upper lip a little higher, creating a decent size opening since She seemed to have a rather large mouth. The EMT then told his assistant to reach inside her mouth and remove her upper set of false teeth.

Sure enough, out came her teeth with his tongue still attached.

Application of a little WD-40 to the teeth and tongue was all it took, and our two classmates were finally physically free from each other. The big question that remains is what did this ordeal do to the budding relationship of the newfound friends? Well, I don't have an answer yet, but both individuals have signed up to attend our next reunion which is now in the planning stages. I am not going to reveal their names, but I will be watching them very closely. Who knows, maybe I will have another *tongue-in-cheek* story to relate to you in the future.

Follow-Up To "The Ties That Bind"

Recently, I wrote about a couple of our classmates whose late evening goodbye kiss after a class reunion turned into quite an ordeal. Well, for those of you who read it, here is a short update:

Both parties have since contacted me and told me essentially the same thing. They confirmed that the story is true. Also, both mentioned that prior to that last reunion evening they had not seen each other in fifty-some years. They also pointed out that they both wear glasses although neither had them on that night. They also pointed out that the lighting in the Wildcat Den was fairly dim and visibility was not the best. And finally, both admitted that the prolonged circumstances of that night triggered emotions and feelings that neither had felt since their youth and both would like to experience again.

But the question came up, how are they to recognize each other so they can perhaps duplicate the event, except that she plans to leave her tongue stud at home? Both swear that although they may not recognize each other for sure, they are both positive they will recognize the sweet taste and ecstasy of their tongues caressing again.

So, I just want to caution all of you, classmates or not, who plan to attend our upcoming reunion: both individuals plan to go around and at every opportunity that weekend stick their tongues into each attendee's mouth until they find each other. Quite a Cinderella story isn't it? So, my message to you is to either keep your mouth shut or carefully choose who you are with when you open it. And beware of imposters. There could be copycats out there.

And finally, if you know of anyone that does not plan to attend the reunion, just let them know what they will be missing. I bet they show up. See you there.

Miracle on Oak Ridge Turnpike

Abraham Lincoln once said, "The world will little note, nor long remember what we say here..." Well, I feel the same way about documenting recent happenings in Oak Ridge, Tennessee, but feel compelled to record the events anyway. Some who were there may take umbrage at my version of events, but they were not observing thru my eyes, which were clear and functioning within the confines of an almost alcohol-free body and a sound mind unaffected by age or overuse. And for those of you who may be skeptical, I also rely on my stellar reputation for accuracy and honesty in my writings. So, here we go. I call the monumental event that I witnessed that late October weekend the Miracle on Oak Ridge Turnpike

It started off simply enough. A few senior citizens, mostly locals, decided to do extra preparation for the Old Folks Convention, otherwise known as a 55th high school reunion, scheduled that weekend. So, on a Thursday afternoon, they gathered together in Knoxville to practice 1) staying up later than usual and 2) finding their way home after dark. I am happy to report that most attendees made it to almost nine o'clock or so before starting to nod off. At that time the designated drivers were entrusted with the responsibility of getting everyone home safely without getting lost. I cannot attest to whether anyone got confused or went to the wrong house (or town) for I did not actually witness their driving. I can report that by Friday afternoon, fifteen or so hours later, everyone was accounted for in Oak Ridge.

Now the convention was scheduled to get fully underway on Friday afternoon sometime between five o'clock and five-thirty. Old folks from all over America plus Kentucky and Alabama were scheduled to open the proceedings with a sedate, low-key meal to be followed by a keynote speech by the public-address announcer at the local football field.

Reunion attendees dancing at the den

How young they felt two hours later

Just let me say no miracles occurred this day. The event was considered a public disaster by everyone in Oak Ridge except the convention attendees. Things went wrong from the start. No restaurant reservations had been made by the event organizers. Folks were confined to making do with whatever food they could rummage up from various sources and eating on the street and sidewalk. As could be expected, some wine bottles and other containers of that ol' devil alcohol started showing up in spite of a local city ordinance prohibiting public consumption within the city limits. My take on the whole scene was that it looked like a bunch of homeless old winos and bag ladies scrambling for a meal and a place to sleep for the evening. Thankfully, the city judge showed up and evidently felt sorry for everyone. Instead of having them arrested, he benevolently joined in the festivities and was generally friendly to all. I did not personally observe him partaking of any alcohol in public.

After the meal, many of the conventioneers walked to the ballpark while others, knowing it was almost dark, returned to the convention headquarters at the Doubletree Hotel. While I didn't attend, I heard the keynote speech lasted over two hours. It appears that the ball field was over-booked and an actual game was being played at the same time. The public-address announcer tried his best, but his speech was very disjointed. It seems he could only talk after each play was run and when the teams scored. Most people came away not remembering a word he said.

To cap off the Friday events, most everyone returned to the convention hotel. Those that didn't fall asleep participated in the hospitality room activities, which consisted of drinks, lies, and 55-year-old background music. It is my opinion that most people in the room were suffering some sort of dementia. The classic signs were there: things such as not recognizing people; talking almost entirely about the past; misplacing room keys; and with misplaced eyeglasses, trying to remember whether they had their clothes on.

The first hint of the miracle to come (or perhaps it had already begun) took place at about eleven o'clock. I didn't recognize it at the time. What happened was the hotel management received a complaint about loud noise coming from the fourth floor and requested the conventioneers to quieten down. This effectively caused the hospitality room to shut down for the evening. Imagine that. Too much noise and too much partying at a time too late for other guests. Folks, at our age this is bragging time.

Saturday was big. Little did we know how big it would be. During free time in the morning, some people toured Oak Ridge. I was surprised at how many searched out their old houses from years ago and had trouble finding them. Perhaps their minds were in worse shape than I thought.

Other folks gravitated back toward the hospitality room. I don't know what attracted them so strongly, but I have some ideas. Putting alcohol, food, and a hundred people in a room the size of some folks' walk-in closets makes for interesting situations. And I confess, I was one of the participants.

The focal point of all scheduled activities was a meal and dance at the Oak Ridge Community Center located on the Oak Ridge Turnpike. At one time this was the Oak Ridge High School hangout called the Wildcat Den. In fact, the main room of the Community Center is still named the Wildcat Den. Dinner started at five o'clock. Everything was cool, calm, and collected but then one guy sort of lost control. Right in the middle of my third slice of pizza this guy jumps on stage and starts singing. He must have thought he was Conway Twi...no, that's not right, maybe Conroy...no, Conrad something or other. Anyway, danged if he wasn't pretty good. I believe he'd make a decent songwriter if he really worked at it. That is something Nashville could use nowadays. But ol' Conrad had done his part. The miracle was underway. (Personal note: Conrad Pierce, now deceased, was a dear and talented classmate who went on to have a successful career in

Nashville as a singer/songwriter).

It was now time for the disc jockey and his dance music. He was named David King when the night started but was called Dancing King before the evening was over. Anyway, let me put things in perspective. Here we have a room full of seventy-something-year-olds. Some still relatively healthy; too many older than their time; feeble; artificial knees, shoulders, and other joints; pockets and purses full of medications; pacemakers; canes and braces; assorted illnesses and heart-related problems; cancers of various types; etc. For those affected, these things were mere inconveniences to be brushed aside this night.

The combination of previous day's activities, renewed and new friendships, the music, dancing, and the general magic taking place at the Wildcat Den was a sight to behold. I watched folks un-age right before my eyes. Folks went from seventy-plus to forty-five to thirty to their twenties within a matter of a couple hours. The ailments of old age had been totally forgotten or at least put on hold for a while. When the attendees reached eighteen, we had to start checking IDs to make sure they were old enough to be there. What a great night. We didn't reminisce about the past or pine for the old days. We made the past part of our present and part of our future. We captured something intangible, something mystical. I cannot explain what happened, but I am fortunate and grateful to be a part of it. To my way of thinking, what took place was truly a miracle on Oak Ridge Turnpike.

At the Sunday morning brunch, I was expecting a tired, weary, relatively small group to show up. Well, what a shock. There was a huge turnout, all bright, bushy-eyed, and eager to further cement relationships before returning home. And I watched many depart and saw something that most people missed. I don't know if it was the smile on the face, the spring in the step, or something else, but I'm pretty certain they left here a lot younger than when they arrived.

Well done, Oak Ridge High School Class of 1959!

The Making of a Legend

Some true stories often have a little fiction mixed in. And many fictional stories often have a little truth mixed in. I will leave it up to the reader to surmise into which category my little tale falls. But I do invite you skeptics to contact the University of Tennessee Athletics Department to verify any of the statistics cited within.

Move over, Jackie Pope. Move over, Howard Dunnebacke. Move over all you ex-Oak Ridge High School football jocks who went on to tote the ol' pigskin at the college level. Oak Ridge had another alumnus that could excel at running with the football. His is a story little known and long forgotten. His is the story of a legend in the making. His is a story that at least one old Class of 1959 graduate has engraved in the sands of time, lest it be inadvertently forgotten in the annals of modern history. His is a story that, had it stayed buried any longer, would have been lost to the fog of advancing dementia; lost to the ravages of long-term alcohol use; lost to the lies of jealous ex-teammates; and lost to a generation that never truly appreciated his accomplishments.

Because others had a much higher profile, he never had much of a chance in junior high or high school. The coaches almost automatically assumed he was not backfield material. They didn't give him a chance at linebacker, corner, or safety. They never even thought to try him at tight end or wide receiver. Punter or field goal kicking was out of the question. Thus, our guy ended up toiling in the obscurity of the offensive and defensive lines. And toil he did. And he did it well.

At the high school level, Oak Ridge was one of the finest teams in the state, losing very few games during the 1955-1958 seasons. Yet in looking back, we can blame those few losses on the coaches. Yeah, most people thought coaches Armstrong and Bordinger were great judges of football talent. Well, time has proved that was not necessarily true. If they were really that good, our guy would have been in the backfield, and we wouldn't have even needed the other backs in most games. Some think if his multiple talents had been recognized at a younger age, Oak Ridge could have played eight-man football. Seven linemen with just him in the backfield might very well have resulted in 10-0 records his sophomore, junior, and senior years. His later record in college strongly supports this thesis.

Well, our guy performed so well that most colleges made the same mistake that his high school coaches did and recruited him strictly as a lineman. And so it came to pass, at the college level he again toiled in obscurity down in the trenches, doing the dirty work while others gained the glory. And in his modest way, he never once complained. But legendary feats were ahead. Fate was about to strike and reveal to the entire world what kind of talent was really contained in this six-foot-two, 190-pound body.

Come with me now to December 2, 1961. Heated rivals the University of Tennessee Volunteers and the Vanderbilt Commodores were locked in their annual battle for bragging rights within the state. But much more was at stake. Bowden Wyatt's Volunteers were struggling to take a step up from mediocrity. A loss in this last game of the season would prevent them from achieving a winning season, both in the overall schedule and in the Southeastern Conference. It would be either 6-4 versus 5-5 and 4-3 versus 3-4.

The game was a brutal battle. Blood flowed in the trenches and pain was inflicted on any carrier who touched the ball. With the score tied at 0-0 and neither team showing any offense, Coach Wyatt tripped over a water bucket on the sidelines and hit his head on the corner of the bench. Arising and shaking off the cobwebs, the coach made a decision that changed history, a decision that had the making of a story for the ages.

"Augustine, you and Richards get in there and generate us some offense."

"But coach, Vandy has the ball."

"Get your butts in there and do what I told you. I know what I am doing!"

And so the legend began.

Vanderbilt had the ball, fourth down and long. Naturally, in a defensive struggle such as this, they decided to punt. At the snap of the ball, Richards was triple-teamed, leaving a huge gap for Pat Augustine to run through, allowing Augustine to make a clean block of the punt. Instantly, Volunteer right guard Larry Richards shed the three blockers on him and, showing no noticeable interest in how bad he had hurt them, scooped up the loose football and headed toward downtown Nashville and the south end zone. Some say the run was more than a hundred and twenty yards. Others swear it was no more than eighty. But all who witnessed it said that he zigzagged the field at least three times, shed 15 to 20 would-be tacklers, left two opposing players with cleat marks on their chests, and waved to his wife Jolene in the stands while signing a couple of autographs at the five-yard line just before scoring the first touchdown of the game. Newspaper reports do not reveal how many times Richards carried the ball after that play, but they do note that Tennessee went on to win the game 41-7.

All that hidden talent of his younger years was finally revealed to the world. Going from right guard to right guy in the right place at the right time, the football lore of Tennessee was changed forever. Move over, Paul Bunyon. Move over, Audie Murphy. Make room for another hero.

Now I am not going to bore the reader with the details about the rest of Larry's career. After all, anyone who wants to research it can find details on the various University of Tennessee websites. But of all the great Tennessee players, of all the great football players nationwide, I challenge anyone to top these statistics for Larry Richards' college career:

1. Averaged twenty-eight yards every time he carried the ball.
2. Scored a touchdown every time he carried the ball.

Tell me, has there ever been another football player in the country that can match accomplishments such as these? Larry deserved better. The media overlooking Peyton Manning for the Heisman trophy pales in comparison to the injustice they did to our fellow classmate and friend from Oak Ridge. It is about time someone set the record straight. It has been my pleasure to do so.

Special Days and Holidays

Remembrance of A Christmas Past

Chapter 1

Private Jake Bowman and Private First Class Duncan McLemore both received the bad news at the same time. Their requests for Christmas leave had just been denied because they were the new men on the post and the two with the least seniority. Besides, they had not accumulated enough leave to go home anyway. And just for the record, they were both nineteen years old, very homesick, and the youngest soldiers in the outfit.

The time was early December 1964, and the place was the Oklahoma City Air Force Station (OCAFS), a small radar site located just outside Oklahoma City near Tinker Air Force Base. Although both young men were soldiers in the U.S. Army, they were part of the Army Air Defense Command's 12th Artillery Group, which was responsible for protecting the mid-south coast from enemy missiles fired toward the United States from the island of Cuba. That put them on an Air Force installation. Army soldiers assigned to the OCAFS monitored dedicated radar screens twenty-four hours per day. Any detected threat of incoming missiles would immediately result in a counter-offensive from Army-controlled Nike Missile Batteries in Louisiana or Texas. The Nikes were highly accurate and fast short-range missiles designed to shoot enemy rockets out of the air before they could land on American soil.

The Army contingent at OCAFS consisted of 60 officers and enlisted men. Only sixteen soldiers lived on post, all young and unmarried. Most were not volunteers. (The highest ranked soldiers living on post were a corporal and myself, a Specialist Fourth Class: same pay grade as a corporal but with no command authority). President Lyndon Johnson had invited us to leave our comfortable civilian lives. He expressed himself in such a manner that he was hard to turn down.

The Army controlled two of the fifteen or so buildings on the station. One was for operational purposes, and one was a semi-converted barracks that contained the Commanding Officer's (C.O.'s) administrative complex, the supply room, and the enlisted men's dayroom on the ground floor. There were eight rooms upstairs that remained unmodified and housed the enlisted men. For those unfamiliar, the dayroom is sort of like a den in a home. It was for use by the off-duty enlisted men and contained a television, a record player, a couple of old sofas, some end tables and chairs, a card table and assorted board games, puzzles, magazines, etc. No alcohol was allowed.

Chapter 2

Private Jake Bowman was a true and proud hillbilly from deep in the hills of western North Carolina. He had never been more than a hundred miles from home before he was drafted into the Army. He spent two days at home after basic training in Fort Jackson, South Carolina, and then departed for duty in Oklahoma, a twenty-six-hour bus ride into land never before seen by him. Jake dropped out of school after the tenth grade to work as a logger and help support the family. He still sent money home each month, although I never knew how much.

Private First Class Duncan McLemore, the youngest of three children, was born and raised on a farm in western Pennsylvania. The nearest town was Bedford, sixteen miles away. Like Jake, Duncan had never been away from home for more than a few days at a time. His father had died of black lung disease shortly before Duncan was drafted. I know for a fact that Duncan was currently sending most of his paycheck home each month. I assumed it was to help his mother make ends meet.

Of those living in the barracks, I was the old man of the outfit. I was twenty-two years old, had been to college and spent a year working in the big city of Washington, D.C. My Army job was that of company clerk, which is probably the best enlisted man's job in the Army. If you have ever watched *M*A*S*H* on television, I was Radar. And I was tight with both our First Sergeant and our C.O.. I don't know why I am telling you this because both denied having anything to do with what happened later.

The C.O. let me go home for two weeks over Thanksgiving in return for me staying on duty over the Christmas Holidays. He told me that two newer soldiers would have to be on duty Christmas Eve and Christmas, and he wanted someone to babysit them. I cannot recall if I mentioned this to any of my family when I was home, so I don't know if any of them were involved in the events that were to come. I do know they all swore they had nothing to do with it.

Chapter 3

It must have been around December 20 when the Greyhound Bus station called and told me a package had arrived, and I could pick it up anytime. Well, of course, I went and got it, assuming it was a Christmas present from home. The box was quite large, about three feet tall by two feet square. There was no return address, but when I signed for it, I was somewhat surprised that it was shipped from Alexandria, Virginia, instead of my hometown of Oak Ridge, Tennessee. But of course! I had a sister living in Alexandria. Her husband was a West Point graduate and Army Captain stationed at the Pentagon. I wondered what she sent that was so large. (When I called to thank her later she didn't have a clue what I was talking about).

In the privacy of my barracks room that evening I tore into the box. Inside was a Christmas tree. Not a real one but an artificial one that looked almost homemade. I don't know how to describe it. It was short and stubby, made mostly of wood with a plastic base and had a burlap-like fabric wrapped around the frame. The fabric had been painted green. Attached to the fabric from top to bottom were all these assorted hand-crafted ornaments, maybe a hundred in all, wrapped in either red, gold, or silver tinfoil. They were obviously made by amateurs. Some ornaments were round, about the size of golf balls. Others were in the shape of matchboxes. Some were tube shaped, about three inches long with a diameter about the size of a water hose. And there was an angel to put on top. This one had an electrical cord and was the only part of the tree that would light up. Let's face it, this tree was ugly.

In the bottom of the box was an unsigned note. It simply said, "*This tree is for the enjoyment only of those who cannot go home for Christmas. When the last off-duty G.I. leaves for home on December 23, place this tree in the dayroom for the three of you to enjoy. Further instructions will follow.*"

Army Air Defense Command's 12th Artillery Group - Author on the left

Ok, who knows only three of us will be here on Christmas day? Who knows that everyone else will be gone on December 23rd? Nevertheless, I waited until all our fellow G.I.'s had departed for home and then placed the tree on a table in the dayroom. That evening, after Duncan and Jake got off duty, I shared the note with them. Jake checked the tree out a little closer than I originally had and commented, "I believe something is inside those ornaments." Upon closer examination, Duncan and I both agreed that he was right. You know, maybe this tree isn't so ugly after all.

Thursday, December 24, arrived and along with the break of day came a Western Union telegram delivered to me by our communications center. It said, "*Your fellow soldiers who live off post will cover for the three of you starting at noon today. Enjoy the afternoon and evening. You, Duncan, and Jake should open your presents from home tonight and open the ornaments on the tree tomorrow morning. The red ones are for you, the gold ones are for Jake, and the silver is for Duncan. Merry Christmas.*" The ink was somewhat smeared, so I could not tell where the telegram originated.

Chapter 4

Sure enough, relief showed up, and Jake, Duncan, and I got off work at noon. We lounged around the dayroom that afternoon, drinking beer that I had mysteriously found iced down in a cooler in my room a little earlier. We had a special time together talking about family, lost loves, hope, and dreams for the future. We also talked about upcoming football bowl games and other important stuff. Through it all, the homesickness of two nineteen-year-olds dominated the spoken and unspoken words of our conversations, and more than one tear hit the floor that afternoon.

I learned that Jake had three younger sisters: eight, ten, and fourteen years old. The fourteen-year-old was crippled from polio. The mother worked at the local community grocery store and typically put in sixty to seventy-hour weeks just to make some extra money. Unfortunately, there was no such thing as overtime. The family was struggling financially since Jake had gotten drafted. He previously made about eighty dollars a week as a local civilian logger and his take-home pay as a private, pay grade E-2, was about seventy-two dollars a *month*, sixty of which he sent home. He had applied for a hardship discharge from the Army but had been turned down. There was no mention of a father, and I did not ask.

Duncan's story was not as dramatic. He, too, had grown up

poor to the outside world but not to him. He had always lived on a farm, so there was always food on the table. He had two older brothers, one of whom was married, and they both still lived near the farm. After his father died, both brothers helped the mother with farm chores and kept the old tractor running. Mom was doing okay. The money being sent home by Duncan was going into an education fund. His dream was to become a forest ranger after he got out of the Army.

In the early evening, I took them to the famous Cattleman's Restaurant at The Stockyards in Oklahoma City for a Christmas meal. It was my present to them. T-bone steaks, baked potatoes, and salad sure beat the cold cuts we would have been served in the mess hall. During dessert, I revealed the contents of the telegram I received that morning.

On the way back to the barracks we drove past a church about the time their Christmas Eve service was starting. On impulse, we joined them and sat in wonder as the Christmas story unfolded. I cannot remember the name of the church but can remember it as one of the most memorable services I had ever attended. Looking back, I'm not so sure it was the service that was so moving. It might have just been an emotional reaction to the special bond that had so recently developed among three friends a long way from home.

That night we sat around drinking more beer, telling stories, and wondering about that tree. Yeah, it was still ugly but in a cute sort of way.

Chapter 5

At seven-thirty on Christmas morning. I walked to the mess hall and got the three of us bacon and egg sandwiches and a jug of coffee. Promptly at eight, the three of us were in the dayroom, curiosity overcoming any urge to oversleep. One would have thought we were little kids rather than grown-up, almost mature adults. And that tree was looking better. Funny how that lit-up angel made all the difference. With no one else around but the three of us, I wondered who had turned it on.

Without ceremony or formality, but with great anticipation, we started to remove and open the ornaments. As instructed, gold went to Jake, silver for Duncan, and red for me. All my ornaments but one contained money. Some had paper money, others contained quarters, fifty-cent pieces, or silver dollars. The one that did not have money contained a simple piece of paper. Cutting through the military jargon, it was orders from our C.O. approving my promotion to E-5 with a corresponding pay raise to a little over three hundred dollars a month. I acted cool but suspect there was a big smile on my face.

Jake's and Duncan's ornaments contained almost identical items. The money they received from many ornaments totaled about $140 each. Remember, this was 1964. For their pay grade, this was equivalent to almost two months' take-home pay. But more important were the other gifts they received. One ornament for each G.I. contained a three-day pass for Tuesday, Wednesday, and Thursday, December 29, 30, and 31, signed by the C.O. Another contained a round trip bus ticket: Jake's to Asheville, North Carolina, and Duncan's to Bedford, Pennsylvania. A third ornament contained a bus schedule and a note from a hometown neighbor, telling them what time they would be picked up on arrival. The buses were scheduled to leave in just a few hours.

Let me explain about the three-day passes. They were for Tuesday, Wednesday, and Thursday. Christmas in 1964 fell on a

Friday. Jake and Duncan were off on Saturday and Sunday. Monday was designated as their day off for Christmas. They were not scheduled to work on Friday, New Year's Day. This meant that Jake and Duncan would be off for nine consecutive days from Saturday, December 26 until Monday, January 4, 1965. Yeah, maybe they would be a day or two late, but the boys were going home!

For two lonely, homesick nineteen-year-old soldiers far away from family and initially not enough money to get home and back even if they had the time, this was truly a gift from God and a Christmas to remember. For the old veteran twenty-two-year-old worldly traveler, his Christmas wasn't so bad either. Otherwise, he wouldn't be writing about it over five decades later. That lump in his throat the rest of the morning was attributed to a coming cold. No sir, no sentimentality for me.

And you know, to this day I still can't get over how good that tree looked!

Chapter 6

Where did that tree come from? Who put the beer in my room? Who decorated the tree and contributed the money and the bus tickets? Who arranged for the neighbors to pick up the G.I.s? I know my C.O. signed the three-day passes and my promotion papers, but when confronted he only said, "Not my decision. Orders from above." All my family and friends professed innocence. The co-workers who filled in for Jake and Duncan claimed the only reason they did so was because they received a revised duty roster ordering them to report to work at 1200 hours. (It was my job to publish the duty roster each day, so I knew that no authorized revision was issued).

Anyway, this concludes my simple little story. Now I am not

going to say there was some sort of Christmas magic involved in all that happened, but neither am I going to say there wasn't. I finally concluded there was just one explanation. Move over, Virginia, I too am a believer.

Epilogue

On that Christmas afternoon in 1964, after I returned from dropping off two friends at the bus station, I stopped by the dayroom. The tree was gone. Instead, I found a note laying on the table that stated, "*My work here is done, I am needed elsewhere.*"

A Secret City Secret

Some people think the Manhattan Project was the greatest secret and scientific achievement in our nation's history. And they are partially right. The effort to develop the atomic bomb and end World War II was indeed shrouded in secrecy and deception, the likes of which mankind has never knowingly seen before or since. Towns were instantly created in the middle of nowhere, appearing on no maps. There was the construction of factories and research facilities faster than ever before in our nation's history. Employees worked for years without knowing what they were developing or building. Houses were erected with their front doors located at the rear so potential spies or mere curiosity seekers would not know who entered or lived there. Key scientists were given fictitious names so they could not be identified by those without a need to know. Security was so tight that you could not even enter the town without passing through guard gates and having official government permission to enter. Well, you get the picture.

It is not my intent here to rehash the history of the Manhattan Project, for it has been well documented elsewhere. Well, almost. There is a story untold that is more unbelievable than the development of the atomic bomb itself. It is a story that will absolutely stun you... if you believe it. I have known about it for four decades and only relate it now because I think you have a right to the real truth, and will treat what you are about to learn with the discretion and sensitivity that is appropriate.

The Mystery Man

In 1939, when Albert Einstein and Leo Szilard sent their letter to President Roosevelt voicing their concerns regarding Germany's progress in atomic theory, an unauthorized male became aware of the letter even before the President received it. Then in 1941, when the President gave the go-ahead for the Manhattan Project, this man's interest became much more intense. He began preliminary planning for a special and secret project of his own. He did not know if he could pull it off but knew the fate of the world was in his hands, and he had to try.

This gentleman, who I will refer to as Mr. X, had an uncanny ability to find out things of which he had no business knowing. And no one knows even to this day how he did it. For instance, when Enrico Fermi demonstrated a nuclear chain reaction at that laboratory under Chicago's Stagg Field, Mr. X knew what had occurred. When General Groves took charge of the great construction project that was to result in the creation of Oak Ridge, Los Alamos, and Hanford, Mr. X quickly learned even the most intimate details. Nothing got past him. It was almost like he knew what they were thinking when they were awake, and knew what they were dreaming when they were asleep.

As the great government project that hopefully would end the war progressed, so did the special project of Mr. X. His project was concentrated in a fairly small area in Anderson County, Tennessee, that was soon to become the home of a town called Oak Ridge. Our mystery man got there before the government did. It is said that strange happenings soon took place on and around a several-miles-long ridge that formed the north border of Bethel Valley and the south border of Bear Creek Valley. Locals called it Polecat Ridge. It is also believed that Mr. X had something to do with the modification of government documents that caused the first experimental nuclear reactor to be built in Bethel Valley instead of at the originally designated site in Hanford, Washington.

Y-12 National Security Complex

Y-12, which was the code name assigned to a huge manufacturing facility during the Manhattan Project, plays a big role in this story. Ever since its conception during the early stages of World War II, the government sold this facility located in Tennessee's Bear Creek Valley as an atomic, and later, nuclear weapons development and production facility. It was supposedly created to help end the great war. In hindsight, if this was true, did you ever wonder why the facility did not shut down after the war was over? Well, I found out why. The government was lying the whole time (or perhaps didn't even know) about the nature of the Y-12 plant. It had nothing to do with weapons of war at all. Oh sure, they did some of that type of work there, but that was just a decoy, a cover-up. The way they compartmentalized everything, none of the thousands of employees even knew what was really going on. This included the guards and security force that protected the plant. That was the mistake that allowed me to discover the real purpose why this vast production complex was built.

Disclaimer

While everything I reveal from this point forward is classified, I am an old man now and do not believe the government will prosecute me. They will assume that no one will believe such a far-fetched story and think of me as a decrepit, senile old codger trying to entertain his few friends left in the world with a tall tale. And while this is true, I know what I know. And I know that many of you readers went to Oak Ridge or other high schools and graduated well before they dumbed down things to the extent that you would believe everything the government tells you. While I think you are safe, read further at your own peril. I cannot guarantee your safety should the government...or others... start cracking down on those who they think know too much.

December 01, 1975

There I was, a dedicated, long-time Y-12 employee working late into the evening, overtime of course, alone in my office when a series of shots rang out. Either the guard force was conducting exercises, or we were under some kind of attack. Within minutes the plant shift superintendent announced on the plant public address system that all employees were to shelter in place and report any unusual activities immediately. Something real was happening!

Minutes later, I heard a loud banging just outside the office. With great intrepidness, I cracked open the door and found a portly, bearded man lying in the hallway with blood running down his face. I'll be frank: though he looked vaguely familiar, I did not recognize him. He was not in his work clothes, wore no security badge, and was a bit shorter than his pictures. But things began to clear up very quickly once he started talking.

His Story

"Son, my name is Nick. I'm going to have to trust you on this. I need help." Then he told me what happened...

His claimed to be on one of his periodic business trips to the Y-12 complex. This year was different. As his transport cleared Polecat Ridge and started its final descent, all hell broke loose. Machine gun fire and surface-to-air missiles filled the air. All of his reindeer suffered injuries of varying degrees. Altitude was lost quickly and in an uncontrollable fashion.

While Nick (I didn't catch his last name) made his way to my office, six of the reindeer allegedly succumbed to their wounds and the other two, uninjured, leaped the electrified security fence and headed for the woods. (The deaths of the six deer were never confirmed and assumed to have been removed by overzealous hunters). According to Nick, the reindeer were part of his backup team and not the first string that everyone knows by name.

The sleigh on which he was riding pretty well disintegrated upon impact. All the guards found during their subsequent search was a pile of firewood. (Further investigation could not later be conducted because one of the guards loaded the wood into a Humvee and took it home later that night to use in his fireplace.)

Santa's Threat

I believed every word that was told to me. After bandaging his wounds, which did not appear to be too serious beyond his broken ankle, I decided to hide him in plain sight. Both Y-12 Security and a first response FBI SWAT team soon arrived to search the building. Nick and I sat in the break room drinking coffee and reading the newspaper during the entire search. We were never even questioned. With all my practice, I knew I could easily pass as an anonymous lowly government worker but was surprised that Nick pulled it off so well. After all, I wasn't totally stupid. By now I figured out that this guy Nick and Mr. X were the same person, better known as Santa Claus.

Anyway, as soon as the search team moved on, Nick implored upon me to get him to the base of Polecat Ridge. As mentioned before, Polecat Ridge is one of the two ridges that parallel the Bear Creek Valley where Y-12 is located. I was very hesitant to honor this request for I was afraid of what would happen when we started sneaking through the plant. Then Santa Claus showed his other face. No longer the fat, jolly old man who goes ho, ho, ho, he threatened me in no uncertain terms. “Jerry, if you don’t do what I say, you will never receive that CB radio and case of beer that you wanted for Christmas this year.” What could I do? My back was against the wall. I did what all good believers do. I took him to Polecat Ridge.

Anyone who believes in Santa Claus believes in magic, and I saw magic performed before my very eyes. Upon arrival at the designated spot to which I had been directed, Nick (or Santa, which is how I will refer to him from now on) removed a portion of the bark from a 200-year-old oak tree and pushed a hidden button. Then it seemed like the whole side of the mountain opened up. We hurried into a huge underground complex, and the mountain closed behind us.

It was at this point that Santa asked if I could keep a secret.

"What choice do I have?" I responded.

"None," he said. "For the next forty years, if you reveal anything that you are about to see here, I will either see that your security clearance is revoked or not bring you any toys."

That did it. My lips were sealed. No way was I taking a chance on not getting any more toys.

Final Caution

Friends, this is a final warning. If you fear for your safety, put this story down right now. Do not finish reading it. Perhaps you can still avoid jail time if the truth ever comes out. Between Homeland Security, NSA, and FBI surveillance, your chances of being detected are minimal since they are all incompetent government agencies. There is some risk, nevertheless. If you choose to go forward, don't worry about the government. Worry about the wrath of Santa should any of this ever be revealed.

The Secret Revealed

We entered that ridge, and my mouth dropped open in awe. I was genuinely stunned. Deep within that hillside was the most massive, modern, and efficient manufacturing complex I have ever seen. Tens of thousands of workers were busy, taking no time to even acknowledge our presence. Millions, or maybe even zillions, of products were being made and packaged at a speed that was almost incomprehensible. Most were toys, but some were other items like CB radios, red Mustang convertibles, and other goodies that appeal to older children; for in Santa's eyes, there are no adults.

Santa was here to check on the progress of his helpers' preparations for the upcoming Christmas. He also checked on his reindeer and his sleighs to make sure they were ready to go. He also had his ankle reset and placed in a cast so he could get along better without my help. Then, with a handshake and a hardy "Thank you," he dismissed me and sent me on my way. I have not seen him since then, but I don't need to. I know he is real. I also know that the way he was treated at Y-12 indicated that he did not have a security clearance. He probably visited too many foreign countries unfriendly to the United States without getting the proper government approvals.

A Few Closing Comments

It is hard to believe that I too fell for the myth just as almost all believers have for all these years. We really thought there was a North Pole workshop up there somewhere in the Arctic. We really thought that somewhere in that frozen tundra of the north, elves were going about their work. The more I think about it, the more it makes sense that Santa Claus was not dumb enough to do something like that. Mr. Claus is one smart man. He pulled it off. His toy factory was located in a warmer climate, hidden from the prying eyes of the world, protected by government guards at no cost to him, and powered by a Department of Energy-owned nuclear reactor located just one valley away. While the reactor was down for service, his underground complex used coal as fuel. During really harsh winters, the bad kids around the world simply got fewer lumps of coal in their stockings. And as an afterthought, I might mention that he was paying no property taxes to the city or state.

Y-12 as a bomb factory? Was that just the cover? President Roosevelt probably knew the truth, but he died suddenly right after approving the Manhattan Project. President Truman was then informed and he also later died. All the great scientists–

Lawrence, Fermi, Szilard, etc.–died or disappeared after the war. General Groves is gone. When you really think about it, the only one left alive who can corroborate my story is Santa himself, and he is not telling.

Now, I personally don't think Mr. X, Nick, Santa, or whatever you want to call him, had anything to do with the deaths of the others, but I am not taking any chances. I have heard and witnessed his tale first hand, and I am a believer. Now that my forty-year moratorium is over and I've passed this story on to you, it is up to each of us to protect both the myth and the truth. We are the only ones left who know that the real North Pole is located in Oak Ridge, Tennessee. The secret of the Secret City is in our hands. Never forget what happened to those who possibly knew the truth early on. I advise you to keep your lips sealed.

Memo to All Those Who Ever Worked at Y-12

As you well know, Y-12 is surrounded by high barbed wire-topped security fencing and other various barriers, most of which are highly classified, to prevent unauthorized entry. If you are not a believer, did you ever wonder where all the deer inside the perimeter came from and how they got there? I have no explanation other than for the fact that back many years ago several deer pulling a sleigh crash-landed in the area. Hmmm, I wonder if they really did die?

MERRY CHRISTMAS, EVERYONE!

Announcement of Change in Employment Status

Posted December 11: Attention, all ladies and other females age 18 and older: I have unretired to take advantage of a new employment opportunity. I will be available around the clock for the next two weeks to verify the adequacy and effectiveness of your Christmas decorations. Please be advised I run a one-man operation and anticipate a backlog. Please schedule my services as early as possible. Due to the nature of my product, males are not eligible for my services.

Fees are negotiable. Each client is entitled to one or more free samples. If not satisfied, I will work to get it right and earn your repeat business. For those not living in the local area, travel arrangements can be made under special conditions. Call for further information. Thank you for your patronage.

Oh, I almost forgot the most important detail. My job title is Mistletoe Tester.

Thoughts of Valentine's Day

Sorry, fellows, this one is for all the ladies in my life... Valentine's Day is an unofficial holiday of sorts that is shrouded in mystery and legend. It is a day of romance and friendship. It is a day for expressing love and affection or hopes thereof. It is a day that kids of all ages send cards or gifts to those to whom they feel some attraction. It is a day for special gifts to those that are just a little more special than others. It is a day when one 76-year-old man realizes there is more than one person in his life that also is part of his heart. It is a day that this man gets to openly express love not only for his wife but for others who are considered more than mere friends.

You have been chosen. I'll not ask you to reciprocate for that would be selfish. I'll not send you roses for roses have thorns, and the petals will wilt. I'll not send you chocolates for candy is temporary. I'll not send you jewelry or other fine gifts for no matter their value, they would not be worthy of my feelings for you. I will send you my wishes for the most special Valentine's day ever. I hope you share this day fully with those you love and relish in the memories of those you love who are not here to share the day.

One can have many valentines. I feel no need to ask you to be mine for you have no choice in the matter. You are already there.

A Sad Valentine's Eve Story

Today, I went shopping for a Valentine's Day present for my sweet wife, Sharon. I got to thinking about how much that woman loves me and how lucky she is to have me. I quickly realized that she deserved something special...not only special but something she would surely want to share with me. Hmm, what should I buy?

Did I say she was lucky? Amen and amen. I racked my brain trying to come up with a gift that could utilize her inherent luck in life to both make her happy and benefit me to some degree. For you see, I love that girl, too. After all, she has lots of money. Most of it is mine. But that is another story.

Anyway, I got this brilliant idea. Now, I am not normally a Lottery player because I never win. But then I am not the lucky one in the family. Knowing Sharon like I do, I came up with the perfect gift.

This afternoon I went to the flower store and purchased this large, three-foot-tall balloon shaped like a valentine and had it filled with helium. I then tied a long string of ribbon on it and tied a clip to the end of the ribbon. Next, I went to the convenience store and bought a fistful of five-dollar scratch-off lottery tickets and clipped them to the balloon. I started getting excited. Anyone lucky enough to land a prize like me and lucky enough to get to trade the home of her youth in the wind-blown flatlands of Tornado Alley for the beautiful hills of East Tennessee has to be a winner.

I just couldn't wait until she started scratching off those tickets. We were going to be rich! And ladies, admit it. Doesn't this sure beat a dozen roses, an ol' box of chocolates or a romantic evening out on the town?

I soon arrived home with my special Valentine's gift. Now, my home has a walk-out basement with a one-car garage where I store my riding lawn mower and other assorted tools. This was a good place to hide my surprise until the appropriate time to give it to her. And so I did, letting the helium-filled balloon float gently upward to rest against the ceiling.

To celebrate my accomplishment, I went down to the beer store and purchased a case of my favorite beverage. Upon arriving back at the house, I pulled into the back driveway near the basement entrance so I could put my beer in the basement refrigerator. Sharon does not allow me to use the one upstairs because she claims my beer takes up too much wine space.

Well, you can guess what happened. I opened the garage door.

There went the balloon. Trailing right behind at the end of that attached ribbon was a stack of scratch-off tickets, still virgin, totally unscratched and valued at who knows how many millions. Like I said earlier, Sharon is the lucky one in the family, not me.

So how much was really lost? Who knows. To quote Bob Dylan or Peter, Paul, and Mary, *"...the answer my friends, is blowing in the wind, the answer is blowing in the wind."*

Tomorrow morning, when Sharon wakes up, and there is no Valentine's present, I suspect she will not be disappointed at all.

After all, she is the luckiest girl in the world. I will still be here, we will still be living in beautiful East Tennessee, and she knows my monthly retirement and social security checks will be here soon. She can just go and buy her own Valentine's present.

Hugs and kisses to all, especially those of the opposite sex.

Valentine's Musings

Ok, folks, Valentine's Day is coming. What are you doing special for this day?

By the way, I just heard the news that men spend twice as much as women on Valentine's Day gifts. That is not true in my household. Sharon spends much, much more than I do. Of course, all the gifts are for herself. She claims her gift to me is saving me the trouble of having to shop for something special for her. Anyway, I have written a whimsical rhyme for the occasion, and though it technically does not fit my usual style, I will share it anyway. It brings back memories of grade school when most of my school friends would always receive more valentines than me.

Bring me your smile, your laugh, your glow;
Expose not the loneliness that only i know.
May one day soon whether we're near or apart,
You'll look deeper to see your name on my heart.
Vibrations of his arrow still quiver within
As the missile of cupid has struck me again.
Love grows stronger or is it hurt that i feel?
Either evokes emotions more intense than mere thrill.
No one but you magnifies this agony and pain

That's accented by my sensing this could all be in vain.
I pray to the gods that my message you'll find;
Note each capital letter then form words in your mind.
Even when deciphered, please don't make me guess...
ease my misery and suffering by just answering "**yes**".

Fallen Warriors

There is a no more mournful, bittersweet, or poignant experience than hearing the sound of Taps rolling across the gentle hills of Arlington National Cemetery. Though you may not see the ritual nor know who is being interred, you know another American warrior has completed the journey and finally found everlasting peace.

I at one time lived briefly in Arlington, Virginia, just across U.S. Route 50 from the cemetery. It was not unusual to hear the bugler's call to Taps several times a day. Occasionally, in the late evenings, I would cross the street and visit the Iwo Jima War Memorial located near the edge of the cemetery. This was my private place of meditation and a safe haven to escape the ills of the world. The cemetery is quiet this time of evening, but most times the silence is louder than any noise from the passing highway traffic. It is a comforting silence and not one of which to be afraid. I thought of myself as an outsider, a mere onlooker who had no personal connection to the souls residing on that hallowed ground. But then things changed. Twice.

The first was Lieutenant Colonel Robert Lawrence (Larry) McCoy, U.S. Army. Larry was a West Point graduate originally from Bluefield, West Virginia. He was a career Army officer and a husband to my sister. The enemy couldn't kill him during his two tours of Vietnam, but the results of that combat got him anyway. They called it a brain tumor, but it had another name: Agent Orange. Over the period of many months, it took him from all-American superhero status to helpless infant unable to think, act, function, or physically care for himself. It was an arduous, heartbreaking, and sometimes bitter struggle that encompassed all involved: Larry, his wife, young daughter, and son. God finally brought an end to his mental and physical pain and suffering.

Let me briefly describe the funeral. While sad, it was one of the most unforgettable events I have ever witnessed. The service started out at a little chapel there in Arlington Cemetery. After the appropriate words by the chaplain, the casket was loaded on the horse-drawn caisson for transport to the grave site. And yes, there was the riderless horse with a backward-turned boot in the stirrup. (Think President John Kennedy's funeral. It may have even been the same caisson and horse.). Traditionally, the family and friends walk behind the caisson to the grave, but I rode in a car due to a leg injury I had at the time. At each road crossing throughout the cemetery, soldiers from the 3rd U.S. Infantry Old Guard Regiment assumed sentry duties as crossing guards to ensure nothing impeded the procession. (Soldiers of the Old Guard unit are

the same ones who guard the Tomb of the Unknown Soldier.). At the grave site the appropriate words were said, and then volleys of shots were fired in honor of the deceased. Taps was played, then the flag was removed from the coffin, folded, and presented to the grieving wife and family.

The thing I remember most about this funeral was the pageantry, the immaculate grooming of the cemetery and the precision, demeanor, and dedication to duty of the soldiers of the Old Guard. I almost forgot I was attending a funeral because their performance was so magnificent. At times I was not so much standing in mourning as in awe at the spectacle I was watching. It took the occasional tear or two dropping from my eyes to remind me of the reality of the event. To this day, I occasionally have guilt feelings that somehow through all the sadness I felt a sense of pleasure at the respect being shown to a fallen warrior. The Old Guard was that good.

Lt. Col. Robert L. McCoy

The second reason that caused my original feelings about Arlington National Cemetery to change was another funeral. He was Jack P. Dove, Captain, U.S. Air Force. He was a fighter pilot and close childhood friend when I was in elementary school in Bluefield, Virginia. Jack was a school teacher who answered the call. He and a co-pilot were shot down in July 1967 over Quang Binh Providence, North Vietnam, probably by a SAM missile. He was listed as missing in action for several years and then finally declared dead by the Air Force. About twenty-five years after being shot down, some remains were found at the site of the crash that were turned over to American authorities. In 1995, testing revealed the remains to be that of both Jack and his co-pilot. Finally, after almost three decades his family had closure to the fate of this American hero.

This funeral was different than those conducted by the Army but was just as impressive. The thing I remember most is what I was told was a "silent sentry." After the service in the chapel, we actually drove to the burial site. Upon arrival, a lone sentry was stationed at the head of the grave, standing at attention to honor the deceased. During the graveside service, the sentry remained motionless, appearing almost like a statue. Of course, when Taps was played, I got my usual chill and tear in my eye. When the service ended, the family and visitors mingled for another thirty to forty-five minutes just visiting with each other. During this entire period, the silent sentry never moved and maintained constant vigilance at the grave. I was thoroughly impressed. By the way, the temperature was in the nineties at this time.

For all I know, that sentry may well still be standing there giving Jack his final protection and respect.

One other interesting thing took place at this funeral. When I saw the size of the coffin, I was shocked. It was a steel box approximately the size of a shoe box and carried the remains of both the pilot and co-pilot. The single marker at the gravesite had both names inscribed on it. I later was told the casket contained only a few small bones, a cigarette lighter and some dog tags. DNA samples were probably used for the positive identification.

My first encounters with Arlington Cemetery were mostly that of a tourist visiting a tourist attraction. It has become more personal since then. I will never think of it that way again. I have finally learned how to keep the purpose of Memorial Day in perspective. Of course, I still plan to enjoy my hot dogs, hamburgers, beer, family, and friends. But I will not forget the family and friends who are not here to enjoy the holiday with me.

Reflections on a New Year's Tradition

For those of you who stay up that late, sometime around midnight on New Year's Eve you might either sing or hear the old folk song, "Auld Lang Syne." Depending on the mood, you might feel pangs of melancholy or nostalgia. You might just be glad it is time to have a final toast so you can now go to bed. You might sing along simply in celebration of an old year gone and a new year beginning. Or most likely, you will sing or listen because it is just traditional or expected that you do so. Well, let me tell you why, if I stay up that late, I will also be singing, off-key and perhaps painfully to others' ears, but sincerely and with different emotions in mind than most of those around me. I might even have a tear or two in my left eye...

Robert Burns first captured the words on paper in the form of a poem way back in the late 1700's. But he didn't originate the words. (It was a traditional folk story even then, having been passed down for generations before him by word of mouth.). It was soon converted to song, and several versions and melodies came to be, but all versions carried a similar message.

Auld lang syne literally means "old long ago" or "days gone by" or "back in the day." The song itself reflects back over happy times from the past, separation from a friend or loved one, then a coming back together again. Some scholars believe the song symbolizes a parting of ways, but they are, in my opinion, in error. It is a work that calls for the preservation or renewal of our oldest, closest friendships. It is a work that highlights the joys and sorrows spent in each other's company and an opportunity for a new beginning. Overall, one can surmise that it reflects on old times with a childhood friend and seeks to revive this feeling of the past by the common modern-day traditions of shaking hands and sharing a drink; a simple act to which we can all relate. I will not recite all the words of one of the more recent translations but offer these three verses for your contemplation:

For auld lang syne my dear,
For auld lang syne,
We'll take a cup of kindness yet
for auld lang syne.
And surely you'll buy your pint cup!
And surely I'll buy mine!
And we'll take a cup of kindness yet
for auld lang syne.
And there's a hand my trusty friend!
And give me a hand o'thine
And we'll take a right good-will draught
for auld lang syne.

Listen to the whole song when you get the opportunity. Then reflect on all your friends, old and new, and the bonds forged during your times together. The words of this oral history from almost three hundred years ago reflect something that is still alive today. How did they know we would still feel this way?

Sometime around midnight each New Year's Eve, I will drink my cup of kindness to those special people in my life in honor and gratitude for our friendship. My smiles and tears will reflect the joy and sadness of treasured memories. And my wish to all will be: *May every New Year be more enjoyable, healthier, happier, and prosperous than the one before.*

Family

About My Wife and Me

Any time one sees the word "Sharon" mentioned in my writings, they need to know I am referring to my wife of more years than I can remember. I still do not know whether her influence on my life has been threatening, intimidating, or inspiring. I will let the readers make that determination. Here is what I can tell you:

In February 1966, two days after being discharged from the U.S. Army, I married a local Oklahoma City girl, and we headed off to Washington, D.C. so I could return to my pre-military job at the Federal Housing Administration. But fate intervened. On the way I stopped in Oak Ridge, Tennessee, to visit my parents. While there I interviewed for a job at the Y-12 National Security Complex, a vast manufacturing and research facility that makes up part of our nation's nuclear weapons complex.

A week after arriving in Washington I received a job offer from Y-12. I accepted and immediately returned to Oak Ridge. Sharon and I have lived in Oak Ridge ever since. I retired from Y-12 a few years ago after a career covering forty-one years and fourteen days.

My retirement plans were to be a kept man, but my wife strongly objected and continues to do so. Not long after my retirement, Sharon chose to go part-time in her job at Oak Ridge Methodist Medical Center where she worked as an accountant. Her decision to cut back was good for her, but it was a *lose, lose* for me. At that time, I became only half of a kept man, losing twenty hours per week of her income. In addition, her decision gave the wonderful wife an additional twenty hours per week of shopping time. For some reason, this meant that she could now spend four times as much money per week. This new math is killing me financially.

But the worst was yet to come. Sharon then decided to fully retire. This, of course, meant the loss of the other half of her income plus another twenty hours per week to shop. I will probably come out of retirement soon as I now require eight times as much money as I did when we were both working. And this does not include any personal spending money for myself. As she tells me frequently, "I'm worth every penny of it!" I certainly agree that she is correct. So are Rolls Royces, Rolex watches, and Twinkies, but I cannot afford any of those either.

As long as the basement printing press holds out I will continue to do busy work around the house, volunteer on occasion, help out at the church, and work in a little travel. I also dabble in a little amateur writing, both prose and poetry. I drink a lot of beer, chase after other women that I am too slow to catch, spend frequent good times with friends, and selectively waste time. At my age, wasted time is not wasted. With family and relatives in Nashville, Louisville, Virginia, West Virginia, Maryland, Pennsylvania, Oklahoma, and several other states, neither Sharon nor I will suffer from a lack of things to do.

Finally, although I have fun at my wife's expense, there is obviously some love there to get us through fifty-three years of marriage and counting. My real goal for the future is to be able to live long enough to start all over and do it all again. I would also like to live long enough to read my own obituary. If I do not make it and Sharon writes the obituary for me, it will simply read:

"Jerry Harris–deceased. I got tired of putting up with his feeble attempts at humor and decided to greatly accelerate the speed of his demise. I did not want old age, accident, illness, or other natural causes to kill him first. I earned and deserved the right to do it myself."

Childhood Memories

Some say it was a simpler time and place. I don't know. From my perspective of a young boy struggling to get out of grade school, life was complicated. I had mom and dad problems, girlfriend problems, transportation problems, and money problems. I also had special friends and that old churchyard, which was more magical than anything Walt Disney ever dreamed up. It is a story worth telling...

I remember some names better than others. There were the Frenchs, the Deatons, Jackie McCormick, and Bobby and Jimmy until they moved away. Then there was Barney and Billy, and several others whose names I cannot recall. And looking back, it seems like everyone had assorted brothers and sisters. They all had a peripheral role to play.

And finally, there was Jack Dove (we called him Jacky back then), who was my best friend in the whole world, and Lynn McIntosh, who was a close number two and almost tied for number one even though he was a Methodist at the time. Between the three of us, we tamed the West, cleared the seven seas of pirates, won several assorted wars, and performed sundry other heroic deeds. If Republic Pictures could film it, we could live it.

It took a Saturday afternoon and time after school during

the following week for us to save the world. Then a new Saturday would bring a new adventure, a new battle to be fought, and a new argument between the three of us. Whose turn was it to be Gene or Roy, or the Durango Kid, or Red Ryder? Who would be Lash Larue, Robin Hood, Dick Tracy, Rex Allen, or Tom Mix? And of course, there were numerous others, depending on who was featured at the Saturday matinee. More about this later, but first let me place it all in context.

The setting was Bluefield, Virginia, in the early 1950s. Our neighborhood generally covered the area going west on Virginia Avenue from Vista Street, past the Graham Christian Church (mine and Jacky's church), down the hill to Cotton's (a neighborhood bar and grill) and Central Cash Grocery, which were located in the same building at the time. From Cotton's, it went east past the Platnick Brothers facility then left, up the hill to Vista Street, and back down to Virginia Avenue. To those unfamiliar, this was an oblong area of a few blocks that seemed a lot bigger when I was a kid than it does now.

Simpler time and place? Those making this claim didn't have to fight their best friend over some third-grade girl who had a crush on both of us. And we both secretly had a crush on her. They don't remember getting cinders in their eyes and hair from that Norfolk and Western Railroad steam engine pulling a hundred loaded coal cars to unknown places. They didn't worry about coming up with an extra penny that awful day when the soda machine down at the grocery store suddenly required six cents instead of five to extract an RC Cola or Nehi Orange. Or having to go to school even though ten inches of snow had fallen during the night; school was never canceled in those days. Or sneaking off and riding a bicycle clear over to Double Gates, only to get a flat tire and have to push it all the way home. (For those unfamiliar with Bluefield, Virginia, Double Gates was the name of the area of town where the golf course, high school, and several subdivisions are now located. It was a highly rural and scarcely populated area back in the 1950s.)

On the other hand, it was a place where even the youngest grade schooler could safely ride a bike to school every day. That was if they had a bike. It was a place where evening entertainment consisted of lying on the floor and listening to *The Green Hornet* or *The Shadow* or *Fibber McGee and Molly* or *This is My Life* on the radio. It was a place that had a train depot. It was a time and place where every night you could see that rotating beam of light that projected upward into the sky from the Beacon Drive-In restaurant. It was a time and place where the grand sum of one quarter would get you into the Lee Theatre for a Saturday afternoon double feature plus cartoon, preview of coming features, and one episode of a serial (ten cents), one popcorn (five cents), one Coke (five cents), with another nickel left over to spend on a toy at the dime store after the movie.

It was also a time and place when the original Graham Christian Church building still stood in all its glory, and a time and place where three little boys ruled the world.

Jacky Dove, previously mentioned as my very best friend in the whole world, lived right next door to the church. I lived at 1008 Virginia Avenue, directly across the street from the Dove's. Lynn McIntosh, the Methodist member of our gang, lived near the top of Vista Street. Lynn was lucky. If he'd lived any farther away, he would have gone to Logan Street Elementary school instead of Dudley Elementary. This would have automatically made him the enemy and assured his expulsion from all neighborhood activities.

The entire neighborhood, especially the area around the church, was our world. Headquarters was in the churchyard. For you see, at the edge of the church property adjacent to Mr. Dove's garage, were three pine trees that had grown up very close together, creating a teepee-shaped configuration with thick green branches from ground to top. Not very noticeable to the eye was a secret entrance, through which we found enough room for the three of us and even a couple of others. It was a place to relax, a sanctuary impenetrable to the rest of the town. It was a safe haven and a place uniquely our own. Just like the Indian burial grounds of last week's movie, we experienced a mystical and sacred feeling whenever we were there.

Now everyone in the neighborhood young enough to know what was really important in life walked downtown to the Lee Theatre every Saturday. As previously mentioned, there was always a western and the second movie would be about pirates, cops and robbers, or some other equally action-packed feature to help mold the minds and values of impressionable youngsters.

Invariably, after the movies the whole gang would go rushing home, eager to choose up sides and reenact the day's events. While the entire geographical area served as a backdrop, most of the action took place on and around the church property. The steps and porch at the front of the church entrance were at times a ship, a castle, a ranch house, a bank to be robbed, and who knows what else. Many a gun battle or sword fight took place around that building. The churchyard served as an army camp, Indian village, ocean, prairie, and many other uses that could only be dreamed up in the minds of imaginative, active kids. Most often, the battles would carry over into the next week, often not being resolved until Friday, just in time to get ready for a new matinee.

Through it all, Jacky and I zealously guarded the integrity of our secret place amidst the pine trees. Other than Lynn, no one else was really welcomed without a special invitation. After all, it was our territory, our place, *our church.*

Well, our private haven served us well. Many times, Jacky or I would run away from home, usually without our parents even knowing. Every time, we headed for that one secluded spot protected by unseen hands from the outside world. Many secret plans and far-reaching excursions originated from within the confines of that treasured cavern. These included squirrel or rabbit hunting with our trusty Red Ryder BB guns and sneaking off to Stony Ridge to hunt for arrowheads. One of Jacky's most brilliant ideas was concocted amid those pine trees. He suggested we talk our parents into letting us sit on a pew by ourselves during Sunday church. When they passed communion, we could help ourselves to as much communion (grape juice) as we wanted. After all, it wasn't fair that adults got refreshments when we didn't. Anyway, the plan worked perfectly except for one thing. The deacon squealed on us. Needless to say, both bottoms got a little sore after church that Sunday.

What a sanctuary those pine trees formed! This was the place we headed to after tossing snowballs at passing cars; this was our private retreat hidden from prying eyes (either Jacky's mother or mine) when we smoked corn silk confiscated from my father's garden; this was the place I sat alone after my grandfather died; this was where Jacky and I picked scabs off our arms and then touched the arms together in the childhood ritual of becoming blood brothers. (This was most meaningful to me since Jacky had real Indian blood. His dad was, if I remember correctly, a full-blooded Cherokee Indian.). This was the only place where we knew we would find safety and comfort, no matter what was happening in the outside world. While our young minds were only just learning about the real purpose of the church and teachings of Jesus Christ, I think our first real feelings of a spiritual nature were formulated on that hallowed ground.

It is interesting to note that throughout those many times we played in the churchyard and around the building, the minister never once asked us to quieten down or leave. Even when we played football or tossed the baseball around, his only words were to "be careful.". Of course, we were never careful, but the good Lord must have been watching over us. We came close many times but never broke a window. It was a place where we were welcomed during the weekdays just as much as we were welcomed each Sunday morning. It was a place where, in spite of our boyish mischievousness, we somehow learned right from wrong and developed strong morals and values. Even now, I wonder on which days of the week we learned the more meaningful lessons of life.

All things come to an end. One fateful evening Graham Christian Church caught fire and was totally destroyed; the building that is. Before a new structure could arise from the ashes, my father got a new job, and my family moved to Tennessee. By then I was an old man of almost twelve. That simpler place and time of my childhood was about to disappear forever. Or so I thought.

I maintained contact with both Jacky and Lynn for a while, through an occasional letter and infrequent visits to Bluefield to visit relatives. But by our junior or senior years in high school, we had pretty well drifted apart, each preparing to make our own way into the world. I was able to keep up with them for a while through relatives and, later on, newspaper articles bringing sad news about Jacky.

It's funny in a way, but it just does not seem like that long ago. Throughout these many ensuing years, I have visited Bluefield many times. Rarely have I returned without driving by the church. On occasion, I have stopped and walked the old neighborhood. Things are different now. The church is much larger, and the sanctuary covers most of the old churchyard. Obviously, the pine trees are gone. The Dove house now belongs to a stranger. But something is still the same. It draws me to that place. Something spiritual.

I have not felt a great need to go inside the church. But I find it more than coincidence that the sanctuary of my youth, for all its changes, is still a sanctuary. Instead of trees and grass, there are pews and stained-glass windows. It is still a place for people to escape the troubles of the world. It is still a place to find joy or to ease the pain of a troubled heart. It is still a place where folks, young and old, learn character and friendship and love.

I have been inside the rebuilt Graham Christian Church only once since I left Bluefield, and that visit was probably forty years ago. I have promised myself that one day soon I will go back. Oh sure, there will be a choir, a pulpit, joyous faces, an inspiring message, etc. But I will look around and see grass, and three pine trees, and feel the presence of two wonderful childhood friends:

one I lost touch with many years ago and one whose presence I last felt at his memorial service and burial in Arlington National Cemetery. And I will feel again the presence of God for–whether in a pew, a churchyard, or sitting in the middle of three pine trees–I will be in His place.

The church members and the pastor will look at me unknowingly and welcome me as a visitor. Little will they know that I am simply coming home.

Kevin and Andy

Some activities between father and son, if repeated often enough, grow in importance in subtle and unspoken ways. I found this out from a particular interaction with the two of you over the years. Call it a special time between a father and son, call it a stupid little ritual, call it superstition, call it a necessary part of preparing for a greater calling, call it a silly little game. Call it anything you want, but do not call it unnecessary. As time passes, one suddenly realizes that the activity is no longer just a random thing that occasionally happens, but a vital part of a yearly quest for perfection strived for often but obtained only once in our time.

You gentlemen are now grown adults with children of your own. It is a time for a passing of the baton, a handing down of a family tradition. It is a time for a new generation of sons to experience the thrill of victory, the agony of defeat, and the challenge of figuring out, "*What part of the tradition did I do wrong?*" when the end result does not go as planned. Your sons have now reached that age. The rest is up to you.

Enjoy this Christmas gift. It may be one of the most thoughtful I have ever given you. Share it freely, but only at the appropriate time, with each of your children. May the results of this new

Jerry and sons Kevin and Andy with Kevin's sons Jacob and Adam on game day

Andy and son Flynn tossing the football

Kevin and son Will tossing the football

generation exceed even those that came before. If not, I will hold each of you boys personally accountable. You are now men in the eyes of everyone except perhaps your father at times, so act like it and do your job.

Dad, Christmas 2013

Explanation to the readers:

While growing up my two sons were avid University of Tennessee Volunteer football fans. We all had season tickets, and before each football game, we tossed a small orange and white rubber football back and forth to each other for fifteen to twenty minutes. This became a game day ritual, and successfully accomplishing this task assured victory most of the time. If our team did lose it was not blamed on the team, it was blamed on one or two of the sons or myself dropping the ball more than once or twice while performing our ritual. If we failed to toss the ball around at all before a game, we were almost assured of losing.

My sons grew up to have children of their own. When the time was right, I wrote this letter to accompany the two new little orange and white footballs that I gave them for Christmas.

A Tribute to My Mother

What a weird woman. She made a career of raising her children. She never worked outside the home. She never learned how to drive. During her first ninety years, she spent only one day in the hospital, and that was when she gave birth to her fifth of five children. She never gossiped nor, to my knowledge, ever said an unkind word to or about anyone. She did not drink, use profanity, run around, or do anything to bring shame or embarrassment to herself or her family. She was a one-man woman and the thought of seeing another man after my father died never entered her mind. She loved her daughters- and sons-in-law as much as her own children. Her church was always a part of her life, and she made sure it was always a part of her children's lives. Yes, indeed, she was surely different by today's standards.

Some may wonder what she did with her free time. Well, while it may be a surprise to most modern women and men, I ask, what free time? Remember that she came from a generation that did not enjoy the modern conveniences that we do. Five kids at home and one of the big events of her life was getting a real refrigerator instead of a new icebox. There were no frozen foods to be conveniently purchased at the grocery store. There was no television to watch, no microwave, no wrinkle-free clothes, no modern washers and dryers, no vacuum cleaner, and for a while not even indoor toilets. VCRs and televisions were unheard of, and even the telephone was a luxury to be shared with several neighbors on a party line. The list goes on....

But there were washing machines with wringers, where each item of clothing had to be hand-fed. The "dryer" consisted of two or three clotheslines strung between poles outside. They worked best when it didn't rain. Ironing was done the old-fashioned way: by hand. And everything got ironed. There were opportunities to have fresh vegetables for each meal, but only because they were raised in our garden, whose tending required no small amount of manual labor on someone's part. Of course, Mom also needed to can what she could for the winter months. Every meal was prepared from scratch, and the dishes were then hand washed. And guess what, she never sent her husband to work or her children to school without a hot breakfast. We all also carried a daily lunch packed by her loving hands. Our clothes were always clean, and we came home every day to a spotless house.

And yes, there was time for entertainment, too: visiting with aunts, uncles, cousins, grandparents, neighbors. Certainly, we children were allowed to go out with our friends at night, but usually on weekends. Weeknights were for family and homework. The nights most fondly remembered consisted of sitting around the kitchen table playing canasta, hearts, or some other game, and just visiting with each other. Other nights were meaningful because we gathered together in the living room to listen to our favorite programs on the radio. Family bonds were built stronger than we ever imagined at the time, bonds that still exist to this day.

As my mother grew older and more feeble, she finally had to give up housekeeping and move in with me, her youngest

The author's mother, Ethel Harris

son. While all her children would have been delighted to have her, my sister Janet and I lived in Oak Ridge, and it was just natural that she should reside with one of us. I was the lucky one because I had more room and Mom felt she would be less of a burden at my house. Burden? Ha! Some of my brothers and sisters have ruefully felt that Janet, Sharon, and myself have perhaps endured more than our share as mother slowed down and suffered from declining health. They are wrong. We have had the pleasure of enjoying these final years to the fullest, and in spite of any health setbacks our mother endured, we have experienced joys, sadness, and a multitude of other emotions that my brothers and sisters (and brothers- and sisters-in-law) have never had the chance to experience. And I feel sorry for them, for it is their loss.

We, the entire family, have been so fortunate and so blessed to have enjoyed, and been loved, and nurtured by Ethel here on earth for most of her ninety-eight-plus years. I feel confident that the Good Lord, too, feels lucky and blessed that it is now His turn.

Beyond the Rainbow

I've got a crazy little story to tell you. One time a year or two ago, after I exited the interstate and was driving those final miles toward a place we have nicknamed The Farm, I saw this beautiful rainbow that looked to be located not far from, and between me and my destination. Now, I say it was a year or two ago, but in fact, it might have been ten or twelve years. Time flies. Anyway, I didn't think much about it at the time. Then suddenly one recent night I had a dream about this rainbow and what it might mean. It bothered me for a few days. The feeling wouldn't go away, so I finally sat down to capture some thoughts on paper. What came from this is a story about a special place and special people, some living and some deceased. It is a story I feel comfortable sharing only with a special few. Hopefully, you won't be too bored...

It is just a small dot on a map. Well, actually you cannot even find it on a map, at least not by name. Use of GPS coordinates might get you close if you're lucky enough to have a satellite signal. The location is in an obscure valley in southwestern Virginia. It is nestled between two Appalachian Mountain ridges which will remain unnamed, mainly to discourage visits by mere curiosity seekers. Some might say it is a place that God neglected. Others might recognize it as perhaps some of His finest work. In support of this latter opinion, what has been widely described as God's Thumbprint can be found just over the mountain.

If you are fortunate enough to be invited, how do you really find your way? Simple. Travel to that little hamlet east of Virginia's tallest town then follow the trail southwest. Local folks call it the Railroad Trail. If you travel far enough, the trail's name will change, but the direction doesn't. Finally, it will end in front of the small house of a single neighbor. Keep going. Just beyond, right on the edge of infinity, is a gate. Go through it, and you will most assuredly experience that calming sense of peace and serenity as you realize you have entered a different time and place: a better time and place, a special time and place. It spans four generations. The woes of a troubled world are left behind.

Turn off your cell phone for the service may be non-existent. There is no need for a television, no newspapers, no mail, and certainly no shopping. Even radio reception is sketchy at best. And guess what? You will not miss any of these items or conveniences. However, you will find a couple of concessions to modern society: 1) A single overhead electrical line strung to the house on the hill overlooking the meadow and 2) indoor plumbing. There was a time that even these didn't exist.

What is there to do in a place so isolated? If you have to ask, you don't belong.

It started out as a place for a few guys to gather during hunting season. But it changed. Or maybe it did not change while those who visited it did. It is a place where children learn character from their observations of those who have come before. It is a place where lifetime friendships are born or nourished. It is a place where boys become men. It is a place where men become better men and, as I have been so aptly reminded, it is also a place where men can go to become boys again. It is a place where one can find quiet solitude but never loneliness. It is a place where the heart can be awed by the wonders of nature. It is a place where troubled hearts are soothed by the loving hand of God. And yes, it is a place where far-flung families can occasionally reunite to strengthen bonds of love and kinship that are too often missing from this modern world.

Although the casual or uninformed reader might not understand, it is also a place where grown men have "ugly" contests, and Leo always wins. It is a place where the same wildlife narratives have been related for forty-plus years by the same tall tale tellers, sometimes called hunters. Amazingly enough, the stories change little over the decades with one exception: the size of the deer and number of tines on the antlers continue to grow with every re-telling. (I heard about a doe shot in 1973 that has since gone through a sex change operation and grown into a twelve pointer.). It is a place where the fireplace consumes more wood in a single November week than is harvested in the state of Washington in a whole year. It is a place where a lot of financial decisions are made annually around a well-used poker table. I've never seen anyone get rich or go bankrupt, but I have seen individual fortunes change by as much as three or four dollars in a single evening. It is a place where the mayor will never be allowed to forget that plate of beans he stepped in so many years ago. It is a place where Mark learned that when lost or confused in the fog, going downhill doesn't always work out as planned. And if the Jones family members were really pressed, they would tell you it is a place where young lads can sometimes provide the appropriate authorities with an excuse to practice their search and rescue operations.

And finally, for a lucky few of us, this small slice of heaven on Earth is almost sacred. It is hallowed ground. It is here that those of us living in the present can renew acquaintances with spirits of the past. This realization happens at the most unexpected moments. One can bend over to drink in a sparkling mountain stream and see the laughing face of Carl looking back. Or look up on the ridge and see Harry walking down the trail still wearing his apron from breakfast. I've heard Frank's name carried on the wind rustling through the trees and often see Sonny in the kitchen cooking another fine supper, or perhaps preparing another special "treat" for someone's bedtime snack. Phlegar is out there too, planning the next practical joke while he sits in that tree stand awaiting that trophy buck. Or that dog. And while I've surely failed to mention some, they will remind me the next time I'm down by the lake, or up at the Settling Pond, or walking the Bulldoze Trail, or climbing East Ridge, or following animal tracks through Corduroy Hollow, or....

They were more than just fathers, uncles, cousins, nephews, grandfathers, in-laws, or friends. Some served one of these roles, and some served many. These were guys that set the hallmarks, the inspiration for those that follow. If the Saints have truly gone home, then home must be here in this place, for these loved ones have not really left us. This is where I find them most often. As for the living, there are certainly more Saints in training. I hunt with them every year. When it comes time for the Good Lord to call them home, I'll know where to find them.

Yes, it is just a small dot on the map. But it is a dot where even Camelot or Xanadu would pale by comparison. The easiest way to find it is in the heart. It lies just beyond the rainbow. A special few made it what it is, and for that, we are truly blessed. They named it Lazy Hollow. A nearby state used to have a widely advertised tourist campaign slogan that read "Almost Heaven.". Well, that state was right. If its next-door neighbor Lazy Hollow was into the slogan business, their slogan would simply state, "You Have Arrived."

Whether from the hills and valleys of Southern Appalachia or from elsewhere in this great land of ours, we all have our rainbows and our special places on the other side. I have found mine. Have you have found yours?

Accidents Happen

As a couple of you know but most don't, my cell phone went to a cookout in Pennsylvania this weekend and allowed things to get out of hand. During the afternoon, the phone inexplicably and without my permission decided to take a dip in the swimming pool. Not only was it not dressed for the occasion, but it also did not know how to swim. Why it chose the deep end of the pool is still a mystery. Having been a dear friend and close companion for several years, I had an obligation to follow and attempt a rescue. And so I did. In fact, I was so fast that I may have hit the water before the phone did. I never saw myself as a hero and still don't. I just reacted naturally and did what any true red-blooded American would do. I knew how to swim. I got out of the water as fast as possible and resumed acting normally. I really don't think anyone else would have even noticed if I had not later mentioned it.

While the doctors have not fully cleared them yet, it appears that my billfold, glasses, and clothing survived the initial encounter. The watch and hearing aids are in Intensive Care, and long-term effects are not yet known. Unfortunately, the cell phone did not survive.

If you have reason to contact me in the next few days, please use my landline. This phone is not allowed out of the house and should thus be protected from the evils of the world.

Nothing Comes Free

I had a blepharoplasty and ptosis surgery last week. You don't know what that is? Neither did I until I complained to my eye doctor about some minor vision loss. Droopy skin and weak eye muscles were the problem. The cure was to have an "eye lift.". Therein lies the problem. It is not as simple as it sounds. Ok, the surgery itself was fairly quick, performed on an outpatient basis, and the recovery has been uneventful. But be very aware of what they do not tell you.

My diagnosis was routine. I took a simple little test, and the doctor looked at me, smiled, and said, "Good news, Jerry. You failed the test. Your problem is functional and not cosmetic."

"Great, Doc. Exactly what does that mean?"

The doctor very carefully explained that the insurance would cover the surgery and I would not have to pay the full cost out-of-pocket. So I signed up. That blankety-blank doctor did not tell me what to expect next. I went home and told Sharon what was going to happen. BIG mistake. Her first reaction was not for my welfare. It was, "Why can I not get this same surgery? I have wanted it for years, but it is too expensive." What was I to do? If I tell her she needs it, death is just around the corner. If I tell her she does not need it, she argues that she wants to look younger, and if I am going to get an eye lift, then she is, too. This discussion is not over yet, but I suspect that my little operation, fully covered by insurance and free of charge, will ultimately cost me $8,000-to-$10,000. Thanks, doc!

Things do not get any better. I get my instructions for the day of the operation. I could not wear clothes during the surgery so I was to show up wearing white cotton socks and white cotton underwear and they would furnish me a gown. They also very specifically told me not to wear my bra or any makeup. If any of you have seen me that early in the morning, you know what I look like without my makeup...and without my bra. While not mentioned specifically, I assumed my silk panties and high heels were to be left at home also.

So I did what they told me to do.

I was scheduled to show up for surgery at eight o'clock in the morning. I arrived ten minutes early, but the surgery ended up not being performed for six more hours. Why, one might ask? I'll tell you why. At exactly 7:57 a.m. I got arrested for indecent exposure. I had on my white socks and underwear just like they told me. How was I to know I was also supposed to wear something else to the office? It was not in the instructions.

After posting $1,000 bail and getting permission from my doctor to put on some clothes, I was released from the jail and returned to the Eye Center where I was now last in line for the operating room. Feeling bad and frustrated about what had taken place, I had two choices: 1) cry in my beer or 2) drink my beer. I chose to drink my beer. In fact, I drank enough of them that when the time for my surgery arrived, I was already asleep and needed no anesthetic. The operation went on anyway and, no joke intended, it left me in stitches; in both eyes, and it was not funny.

Well, a few days have now passed. The bruising around the eyes has faded. The swelling has subsided. The city judge dropped the indecent exposure charges. The good doctor has returned the two beer cans I had not drank when I passed out. The only problem is, both are empty. I wonder if he drank them before or after he operated on me?

As I mentioned, insurance will cover my surgery. To cover my cost for the beer, I wonder if the good doctor will be willing to knock a few bucks off the cost of Sharon's potential upcoming procedure?

News Release

Because of my strong and, in my opinion, correct opinions on a variety of subjects, many of my friends are constantly urging me to run for public office, usually *President of the United States*. My hesitancy to do so often results in impromptu but vast grassroots efforts to draft me as a candidate. As much as my country needs me, I refuse to lower myself to the standards required to be a politician. Therefore, I have prepared the following statement to clarify my current position:

OFFICIAL STATEMENT - FOR IMMEDIATE RELEASE
I'll limit my remarks to a few brief sentences while making all of my positions perfectly clear. As a liberal-leaning tea party socialistic progressive conservative who believes in both pro-choice for women and right-to-life for the unborn child, I strongly believe that a good democratic republican should be independent enough to favor a single-payer universal government health care program provided by free market capitalistic principles at no cost to the consumer or taxpayer, assuming we balance the budget no matter how much it costs or how much more we have to borrow to underwrite all current and future social and welfare goals while reducing taxes and paying off our national debt. Furthermore, I believe

we need to confront the war on poverty, the war on terror, and the immigration issue with all the resources this great country has to offer as long as we don't have to spend money or offend anybody and not have to ask our fellow and sister citizens to choose between political correctness and common sense. After all, a couple of major goals are to totally wipe out ISIS and the threat of radical Islamic terrorism from the face of the Earth without harming anyone or violating anyone's religious principles and to seal the borders without preventing anyone from entering the country for any reason.

After thoughtful consideration and consultation with my family and friends and to protect what little reputation I have left, I am withdrawing my name from consideration as a candidate for the office of President of the United States. Please withhold your donations to my campaign unless they are large enough to tempt me to change my mind. May the second best candidate win.

Friends and Birthdays

Two Too Many—
A Personal Letter to the Twins

I can only imagine the confusion that identical twins suffer throughout their lives with people not being able to tell who is who or which is which. For you guys, however, it must be worse than normal. I have reached the conclusion that even the two of you are not sure at times. I was always under the impression that Mark was older and I was going to send my findings to him first, but I accidentally learned that maybe I was wrong and that Steve was really the oldest. I also learned some other things. Well, perhaps it was more speculation than fact, but now I am unsure what to think. It all happened like this:

I was visiting a nursing home last week and met an old fellow around 115 years of age. He was lucid most of the time, but I could tell the ravages of old age had taken a toll on his mind. He related to me an unusual tale that, while I was skeptical, did make a little sense and I want to pass it along to you. The old guy was a doctor in his younger days and delivered many babies in his time. One particular set of twins, however, was what he remembered most...

Mrs. Croall was rushed to the hospital with fairly significant labor pains. Our doctor delivered a fine, healthy set of baby boys without incident. Then he went to fill out the birth certificates. He listed the name "Mark Croall" for the one who arrived first and the name "Steve Croall" on the one who arrived last. He then went to the hospital room where the doctor was to present the proud parents with the records of birth. But then the doctor got confused. He looked at the two boys in their mother's arms and could not tell which was which. Maybe Mark was really Steve and Steve was really Mark. The doctor returned to his office with the intent of reissuing the birth certificates with the names reversed. The first thing he did was stamp a big red "X" on the original documents to indicate they were null and void. Then he was interrupted and had to rush off to attend to an emergency, forgetting all about the birth certificates. A nurse found the original certificates and thinking they were complete, gave them to the new mother and father.

When the proud parents examined the certificates, they noticed that one was for "Mark CroXall" and the other was for "Steve CroXall. Noticing the different last name and not wanting future teachers and friends to think these boys were illegitimate or adopted, Mr. and Mrs. Croall immediately had their last name legally changed to Croxall to prevent any confusion.

To make matters more complicated, the old doctor related to me that around nine months before the boys were born, the mother had suffered a bad accidental cut from a kitchen knife that had pierced her lower abdomen. The mother healed up just fine, but Doc was still concerned. He suspected it had severed one of the genes that were fundamental to the mother's ability to give birth to children. The doctor later surmised that maybe Mrs. Croall was already pregnant at the time and what may have really happened was that the tiny spark of life in her body was cut in half but continued to survive. When Mrs. Croall later had her twins, the doctor was even more perplexed. Although it had never happened before in history, there was a real possibility that Mark and Steve were not twins at all but one person who simply had the misfortunate to be divided in half immediately after conception with each half growing separately. In this case, both of you should carry the same name and maybe could be Part 1 and Part 2. Could this be why you two have grown up kidding each other that "While I still love you, brother, you're only half the man I am."

I don't know where the truth lies and I suppose it makes no difference. All I can do is hope the two of you are at ease with who you think you really are. And Mark, if you are really Steve; and Steve, if you are really Mark, it makes no difference since I cannot tell the two of you apart. I wish the four of you the best. It looks to me like double the fun is the order of the day. Enjoy it to the fullest.

Truth or Fiction

This world is getting so crazy that I have stopped trying to separate truth from fiction. Just basically being a simple ol' country boy from the South, I have learned to go on my first impressions, right or wrong. And no one can change my mind. At least while I'm not naked, still sober and fully clothed.

Now with that disclaimer out of the way, let's talk about a specific classmate of mine: an individual who has greatly changed over the years. Trust me on this. One good look is all it takes to read a person. I learned long ago not to judge a book by the cover, but at least check out its contents first...or second, if the book happens to have a centerfold.

Well, I have skimmed over a few pages and formed a few impressions. First, he ain't one of us, not anymore. Applying common Redneck Reasoning, here is what I have discovered.

1. He is college educated, which automatically makes him think he is smart. He flaunts his ability to write in cursive, spell the words correctly, and then demonstrate the ability to read them back to you.
2. He has spent most of his adult life living in the city.

3. He pours his "likker" out of a bottle with a tax stamp on it. Then he drinks it out of a glass. Compounding the problem, it looks brown or amber instead of white like ours. I wouldn't be the least bit surprised if it were made out of rye or some other fancy grain instead of corn.
4. He wears khaki pants, shirts with button-down collars, and colored socks. He owns several ties and blows his nose in a fancy handkerchief instead of on his shirt sleeve. I'm willing to bet that he doesn't even own a pair of overalls. Even if he did, he is the type who would probably dry clean them.
5. "Muskeydime" wine is not good enough for him. He drinks that sissy stuff colored "red" or "blush" or sometimes "white," which really is the color of squirrel urine. I even heard him one time call the wine he was served "Yellow Tail."
6. He wears deodorant. And he usually takes showers before applying it even if it is not Saturday night.
7. He trims his beard.
8. Most damning of all, his family is not good enough for him. Can you believe he actually married someone who was not kinfolk?

But there is hope for him yet. He belongs to a clan, members of which at one time lived on or near Black Oak Ridge. In fact, some of them gathered down at the big lake in Gulf Shores, Alabama, this week and he showed up. And guess what? He actually drove a car instead of a pickup truck. But he still knew where Oak Ridge, Pine Ridge, and Pine Valley are located. And just as we find him different and much changed over time, I suspect he feels the same about all of us. You know what? Clans in the South are like families: No matter how different you are, you still belong.

Tribute to Another Tennessean in Texas

Back in October 1843, that great Tennessean named Sam Houston led a group of Texas commissioners that signed a treaty with ten Indian nations. The meeting took place at a little river site called Grape Vine Springs. This opened the entire Grape Vine Prairie to homesteaders who flocked to the area. Soon, a thriving little settlement sprang up and, naturally, it was called Grape Vine. Most likely the name "Grape Vine" originated from the wild grapes that were native to the region. In spite of the name, it was cotton and then later cantaloupes that made the Grapevine Valley prosper. In fact, as late as the 1970s Grape Vine was known as the Cantaloupe Capital of the World.

But things changed. Another great Tennessean, Jo Ann Cavosie Moore, moved to Grape Vine, Texas. The cotton went away, and the cantaloupe production dropped significantly. Now there is no written record to show that Jo Ann met with any group to change the course of history such as Ol' Sam did way back when. She is a quiet, shy person who shuns the limelight and freely shares credit with others. But here is what transpired in her community after her arrival: 1) The consumption of wine went from a mere trickle to volumes beyond all imagination and 2) enterprising landowners and businessmen remembered the reason for the name of their town and realized that grapes would still grow there. Whether under Jo Ann's guidance and direction or not, at least eleven wineries and vineyards sprang up, some literally overnight. These include LaBuenia, Bingham, Cross Timbers, Su Vino, Delaney, Umbra, Homestead, Farina's, Messina Hof, Wine Fusion, and Sloan and Williams.

With the wine production exceeding what one would expect in her fair town, I must assume Jo Ann Moore had some help and was not drinking that much all by herself. Regardless, either due to all the wineries or simply due to her and her husband's residence there, Grape Vine, Texas, is today considered one of the most desirable places to live in the United States. In honor of her accomplishments in developing the local wine industry and the fact that another Tennessean has made history in Texas, it is my distinct honor to recognize the magnificent accomplishments of a Tennessee woman from the Atomic City.

Congratulations on a well-deserved honor, Ms. Moore. And if you ever wonder where I got all my information...I heard it through the grapevine.

Presents for Girlfriends

To all my girlfriends, your birthdays have caused me a big problem, and for this, I apologize. Let me explain:

I had three major places of employment during my career: Federal Housing Administration, U.S. Army, and the Y-12 National Security Complex. All of these places were supported by federal (taxpayer) funding. You contributed to every paycheck I drew. Then, after I retired, I started drawing a pension from Y-12, again underwritten by you and other taxpayers. I cashed in a few savings bonds, interest compliments of the government (taxpayers). And I started drawing my social security check. Now, I paid into social security all my life but of course, the money was taken out of my paychecks, and you remember where my paychecks came from! Before I go any further, thank you very much for supporting me all these years.

Anyway, when I realized your birthdays were coming up, I got to thinking, "*In a sense, these girls own a big part of me. It is only fair that they get a wonderful dividend for this lifetime investment.*" After birthday shopping for each of you at the jewelry store, I went to pay the bill. That is when I realized I had a problem. You see, I am married. All that money that I thought was mine all these years went into a joint checking account. Need I say more? While

Sharon is doing well, I found out I am flat broke and can only send you my fondest wishes that you have the happiest of birthdays. And once the partying is over and things again settle down to normal, if you and your fellow and sister taxpayers can find it in your heart, I need a raise.

Outer Banks Report

In August 1587, a small group of about 115 English settlers landed on Roanoke Island in what is now the Outer Banks of North Carolina. The leader of the group, John White, had to return to England a few months later. Due to circumstances beyond White's control, it was August of 1590 before he was able to return to Roanoke Island and the family, friends, and newborn child he'd left behind. Unfortunately, upon arrival, he found no trace of the colony nor any of the inhabitants and almost no clues as to what could have happened to them. This group of settlers came to be known as The Lost Colony, and their fate has been a mystery for more than four hundred years.

In May of 2014, a small group of twelve revelers, old friends with roots in Oak Ridge, Tennessee, landed at Nags Head, North Carolina, just a stone's throw or two from where the Lost Colony first settled. Rumor has it that this new group of motley upstarts was a secretive, close-knit group that tended to shun outsiders. They mostly associated with those coming from similar backgrounds and sharing similar interests. Allegedly, they performed certain rituals such as sleeping, eating, partying, drinking, shopping, and exploring local sites together. Either by design or fate, they left some of their own kind behind (at home) to carry on the traditions in case this group of twelve should also suffer the same unkind fate as those who came before.

Well, I was there in Nags Head for a short period of time, and I can only report what I saw with my own eyes or heard with my own ears. Let me say up front, the rumors were for the most part true. Clues were left behind this time: numerous empty beer, wine, and vodka bottles; scuff marks on the floors, possibly caused by dancing; food crumbs all over the living room and kitchen, analysis of which indicated that gourmet meals were supplemented by late night snack food; guitar picks that at first glance looked like they may have been left by some Nashville-based entertainer that some claimed was from the Class of 1959; neighbors that swore they heard music by Timi Yuro, Jerry Butler, The Drifters, and many other 50s and 60s artists, all of whom were singing backup to nightly live performances by one or more of the house occupants; tongue imprints on several glasses, indicating that the contents, consisting of either cosmopolitans or margaritas, had been licked dry. A few hair rollers were found at the scene, indicating a whole lot of primping going on. And yes, there was a shopping bag or two.

There was evidently some interaction between the group and local natives. Articles in The Nags Head Times reported that several natives named Kay, Sara, and Wanda all survived their encounter with the group, suffering nothing more than prolonged and memory-fogging hangovers. The news article also mentioned that the encampment of the visitors interrupted the sleep of neighbors until long after midnight on Monday, until 11 p.m. on Tuesday, 10 p.m. on Wednesday, and 8:30 p.m. on Thursday. No births were reported during this time. It is thought that this group of outsiders practiced the ultimate form of birth control. It is called Age. Their tendency to go to bed earlier each night than the night before is not understood at this time. My personal observations are that the length of time for hard partying each day remained the same. They just started earlier each morning, allowing them time to finish earlier each night.

By Friday, May 09, 2014, most of the group had disappeared. Three remained behind, but by the next day two of those were gone, and the third was missing. It is possible that she still remains in the Outer Banks area, but there is no real evidence to confirm this. History will record the events of this week as a special time, and the group will be named, with apologies to Ronnie Milsap, as The "Lost in the 50s Colony." Will it be four hundred years or more before we know what really happened? Perhaps so, perhaps not. All that I can promise Relma, John, Linda, Kathryn, Steve, Betsy, Jim, Cyndi, Joe, Gloria, and Sharon, is that I'll never tell.

Miller Time - Personal Comments to a Friend

Way back in the 1200s, I believe it was King Edward the First who introduced personal taxation. This created a situation where the populace was required to have surnames. Well, the guy who ran the local mill that all the farmers used to grind their corn was called Henry, or Joe, or whatever. Thus it was natural that the surname for him and his family became "Miller.". So for tax purposes, he was now officially named Henry Miller, or Joe Miller, or Whatever Miller. And there must have been a heck of a lot of mills in Olde Scotland since there are more than forty coats-of-arms today that bear the Miller name.

Tom Miller, I have often wondered which clan you came from. There was a group of musical Millers that eventually sired Glenn, who formed a band in 1938, Big Band so I understand. He went on to have fifty-nine Top Ten hits between 1939 and 1942, and later took one plane ride that he shouldn't have. Then there was a group of Millers who knew how to write, one of whom had a son named Arthur. Arthur wrote Death of A Salesman around 1949, but his greatest fame came from marrying Marilyn Monroe in 1956. Another writing Miller was named Henry. His two most famous novels were *Tropic of Cancer* and *Tropic of Capricorn,* both of which, because of their explicit sexual content, were banned in the United States for more than three decades. And then there was that group of funny Millers. After centuries of trying, they came up with a clown named Dennis. Dennis was one of the early comedians on *Saturday Night Live*, won a couple of Emmys, and often appeared on Fox News' *Bill O'Reilly show.*

None of these Miller clans seemed right for you. However, I found the one that I like to think if you traced your ancestors back for many generations, would fit the profile I envision for you. Fred Miller (the formal name was actually Fredrick) remained a dedicated miller throughout his entire life. Even after the days of the mills had passed, Fred remained committed to keeping the grain business alive and giving the farmers a place to sell their barley, wheat, etc. Fredrick purchased the old Plant Road brewery, changed its name, and in 1855 produced his first keg of beer. His business is still thriving today. Just think of how many farmers have been employed over the years, providing his beer factory with needed raw materials, and just think of how many taxes he has paid to the king and other government representatives.

Fred was my kind of man. He lived the High Life, and that is just what you deserve. I understand that December 2 is your birthdate. From this time forward, the twenty-four hours that comprise December 2 will forever in my mind be named in your honor and will be recognized by others throughout the nation. We call it Miller Time.

Mack the Knife Revisited

I was driving to the store yesterday and turned on my truck radio. My grandson had driven the truck recently and had the radio dial set to some station that plays music that was unrecognizable to this old man. It wasn't *country*. It wasn't the *rock 'n' roll* that I remember. It wasn't *folk*, *jazz*, or *opera*, and it wasn't *popular*. This unpleasant noise blaring out of the speakers was in fact merely painful, but very short lived. I had fortunately caught only the last several seconds of what the disc jockey claimed was the Number One song of the week. I darn near broke my finger punching the button to change the station, but it was worth it.

My experience had nothing to do with the 1950s, but somehow I got to thinking about high school friends and started reminiscing about our high school days. I wondered out loud if they could still remember back that far. Well, if you are one of us and are reading this, let me help you out. At this exact same time of the year in 1959, there were some folks who became popular that you may or may not remember. Do you remember Louie Miller? Well, he disappeared, babe. And what about MacHeath? He used to spend just like a sailor. Then there was Jenny Diver, ho, ho, yeah, Sukey Tawdry, ooh, Miss Lotte Lenya and old Lucy Brown. Surely you remember them. And to top it off, for many weeks in

1959, Bobby was The Man. He had the Number One song in the nation at that time. He even warned us: "Ya know when that shark bites with his teeth, babe, scarlet billows start to spread." (You guys do know what a billow is, don't you?). What more can I say? Ol' Macky was back in town.

I channeled Bobby today, and we reached a mutual agreement. The two of us plus Louie, MacHeath, Jenny, Sukey, Lotte, and Lucy all wish you folks were here with us. In celebration of enduring friendships and in fond remembrance of our high school days, Bobby and I are going to cut class this afternoon and go over to the Midtown grocery store and find somebody old enough to buy us a fifty-cent quart of Falstaff. We'll drink it in your honor while riding around and playing some real music on the car radio.

Ol' Macky is back for some and never left for others. Memories are as great as you make them. Ride those billows of life with a smile on your face and music in your hearts. Celebrate like you are seventeen again! Your fellow and sister Old Timers will be there in spirit celebrating with you.

Kathy Comes Home

I don't know whether it is originating from the Oak Ridge National Laboratory, the Y-12 National Security Complex, or some other unknown place here in the Atomic City. All I know is it functions much like a homing beacon. Many of those who lived here before, especially those from the late 1950s, feel its power. Like a magnet or some sort of unexplainable force field, it calls them back. Most have felt it, some much stronger than others. Some have yielded while others continue to resist. It is mysterious. It is eerie. It is beyond common understanding. Some say it is not of this world. And for those who yield to its drawing power, it is perhaps magic. I will not try to explain it, for it is beyond my comprehension. But I can tell you a little story...

She was just a little old lady from the Class of 1959 who had moved away long ago. While names are not important, most of us knew her way back then. You know, before *the change*. Well, like many of us fully understand, time has taken its toll. She indeed changed and, many said, not for the better. Oh, she struggled to stay active over the years and hid her ailments well for the most part, but the aging process could not be denied. She fought the good fight as long as she could, then made the fateful decision.

She felt it but didn't recognize it for what it was. She mistook the mystic drawing power of the unexplained force from a small community in East Tennessee for mere wanderlust. She fought her natural instincts and headed in the opposite direction. With stubborn resolve, she boarded the Queen Mary 2 and made it as far as England before the force weakened her resolve. Trying her best not to give in, she tied herself to a bed in a downtown English hotel for five days until finally, in her anguish, she was compelled to yield ground. Fighting the overwhelming forces trying to take control of her body, she eventually found herself back in the United States. Struggling to keep the force from taking control of her mind also, she fled to the so-called sanctuary of the Outer Banks in North Carolina. That did not work. That beacon was calling, and she was weary. Giving in to the inevitable, she gave herself up. She went home–the old home–the home of her teenage years, the home where she was exposed to radiation fields and utmost secrecy and unknown happenings in the mysterious production plants that surrounded the city. It was the old homeplace where she was exposed to memories and history and friendships that have surpassed all generations since. And most important, this return to the hometown of her younger days did something more astounding and powerful, more unbelievable and more magical than any of you could ever accept, except for those of you who still live in Oak Ridge. You know what I am talking about.

I had the privilege of spending her birthday eve with Kathryn Horne. She had totally given in to the greater power that had brought her home. And in this surrender, she was set free. Right before my eyes, she lost four or five decades of age. She became giggly and cute in that little girl way and looked so young that an identification card was necessary for her to prove she was old enough to drink the wine in front of her. And even at that, she had to lie about her age to be served. And I soon realized that she was truly our kind of an Oak Ridge girl. The sun went down but, thanks to Kathy, the darkness stayed away. I thought I had noticed a glow about her earlier, but it was now confirmed. She truly did glow in the dark.

Today is Ms. Horne's 21st birthday, and she does not have to lie any longer. She has finally yielded to that force that has been calling her back. And for those of you who do not live in Oak Ridge, I am going to reveal my theory on where that unknown but all-powerful force originates. To use yesterday's terms, it is not Y-12. It is not X-10. It is not K-25. (These are Manhattan Project code names for nuclear facilities in Oak Ridge.). In my opinion, it is a place called Oak Ridge High School at a time that was special and surrounded by classmates that were even more special. Kathy, thanks for being part of our past, present, and future.

Jack is Standing Tall

One of the great symbols of our country is the magnificent U.S. Capitol Building, recognized throughout the world and representative of all that is right and good in this vast section of our universe. I don't know how much attention most of you have paid, but if one looks at the Capitol very closely, standing there at the very top of the dome is a statue, nineteen and one/half feet tall. This statue overlooks our great land of the brave and the free. It is simply named the Statue of Freedom.

Well, I got to thinking last night. Who in the world stands nineteen and one/half feet tall and weighs 15,000 pounds. Then I thought about the Oak Ridge High School Class of 1959. Over these many years since our graduation, many classmates have obtained this height and some even more, at least in stature. And even with all the pounds some of us have put on, we, fortunately, do not weigh that much...yet.

Then I got to thinking, maybe the old gal at the top of the dome needs some relief every now and then. Why don't we pick a day and have a class representative stand up there in her place? Hmmm, what day would be best and who should we choose?

Jack, I've got to tell you, you were not the first choice. In selecting someone for this honor, there were a couple hundred eligible candidates, and most of them tied for first. I excluded myself because I am both shorter than nineteen and one/half feet in stature and afraid of heights.

I looked up the specifications on the dome and found out the top was not large enough for a whole bunch of people. The huddled masses could not make themselves that small. Ok, how do you pick one representative from many equals? Well, I'll tell you how: accept bribes. And that was the tiebreaker. Certainly, a man of your integrity would not resort to bribes, but someone did in your name. They submitted seventeen cents, and that was fifteen cents higher than second place. Dare I say that whoever submitted you name got their two cents worth!

Congratulations, Jack. You won. Anyone who visits the capitol today and looks up or anyone who views a photograph taken today of the Statue of Freedom may notice something a little unusual. The face will be different, the height may be a little higher, and if one looks closely enough, I do believe the figure on the statue will be wearing an Oak Ridge High School Letterman's jacket. I have written to the President of the United States and suggested we make this change permanent.

Jack, we raise a toast to you in honor of this occasion and many years of friendship; we may not be there physically, but we know where you are. As I raise my eyes to the top of the dome, I am happy to report the Statue of Freedom is standing tall today.

Comments and Advice to a Friend on a Day of Celebration

Forgive me if I get a little *long-winded* or sound like a *smart aleck* delivering a *tongue lashing*, but the *ugly truth* I am about to discuss is *pretty awful*. (And by the way, if two people tongue lash each other, are they French kissing?).

Sometimes in exercising the English language, we use words that make absolutely no *dadgum* sense relative to the subject, and we are either too stupid or too smart to realize it. It is a good thing we do not interpret words literally. It is *clear as a bell* that if we did, we could not believe anything we read, hear, or say. Or maybe bell is the wrong word to use. Perhaps it is merely *clear as mud*. For instance, I find myself *between a rock and a hard place* today. I would *give an arm and a leg* if I did not have to be a *fuddy-duddy* and *spill the beans* about this *red-letter day* of yours. Now I have *no ax to grind*, but it is more than *lickety-split* time for some of your friends to *face the music*. Many of those who take time to wish you a happy birthday today have either *gone bananas* or *have bats in the belfry*. Those *old geezers* make me *sick as a dog* the way they think. (Are female geezers called geezerettes?)

Now I don't mean to *get your dander up*, but it is *easy as pie* for your friends to erroneously go all out and wish you "happy birthday" greetings. Well, to *coin a phrase*, it is a *no-brainer* that these *well-heeled* friends of yours are *off their rockers*. The only birthday you ever had was over three-quarters of a century ago. They need to quit *talking through their hats*. Let's get down to the *nitty-gritty*; all celebrations that have followed that first one are not birthdays...they are anniversaries!

Please don't get me wrong, I would be *happy as a clam* to *climb on the bandwagon* and not engage in *double talk* like they do, but their *run of the mill sound bites* are nothing but *smoke and mirrors* from a bunch of *loose cannons* that have either *lost their marbles* or simply do not understand the true meaning of the written word. I bet that if I asked them to *spill the beans*, they would not know what I am talking about. They would think I was either trying to *get their goat* or else that I was *off in la-la land*. If I engaged them in conversation and tried to explain myself, I would probably be accused of *chewing the fat* or just *shooting the breeze*. No matter how irritated I get, I refuse to have a *conniption fit*. But neither am I am going to debate the point any longer–no more *dilly-dallying* around. They can either *put this in their pipe and smoke it* or else *hit the road*. Better yet, they can *smack dab* do both.

So let me get to the real message that I am trying to relay to you. *Time has run out*. I cannot *kick the can down the road any longer*. Today is a special day and one you should celebrate to the fullest. From the time your alarm clock notifies you to *rise and shine*, I hope you reach for *that pie in the sky*. Hopefully, before your birthday anniversary celebration is over tonight, you will have lived *high on the hog*, obtained your most desired *pipe dream*, had at least one *square meal* featuring the *flavor of the month*, and enjoyed a *wild and wooly* time. And if for some reason you do not get the *whole shebang* or *kit and caboodle* this year, do not *fly off the handle* and come *crying on my shoulder*. You'll be *barking up the wrong tree*. There is always next year. Remember, life's little adversities just reinforce the fact that sometimes you just *cannot have your cake and eat it, too*.

And if, *whoops-a-daisy*, you should get picked up by the *long arm of the law* while celebrating, just *play it by ear* and don't have a *hissy fit*. Take *the high road* and, if you are lucky, things will not go completely *haywire*, and you will be able to *walk a straight line* and continue your *fifteen minutes of fame* without having to face a *kangaroo court*. The results of these can sometimes make one *hopping mad*... or worse. You could end up in the *clinker*. This would put you *up the creek without a paddle* and probably result in a little unwanted *downtime*.

Off the top of my head, my final advice to you is: if you drink the nectars of the gods freely today, *have a blast*. Just remember to *live it up* with caution. Otherwise, you might have to *live it down*. At the end of the day, may everything be *hunky dory*. Enjoy a good night of peaceful sleep. And may those that celebrate with you not deliver a *double whammy* and insult your intelligence by accusing you of getting *drunk as a skunk* then passing *out like a light*. If they do, tell them to *go to hell in a hand basket* or simply *flip them the bird*. After all, *a bird in the hand is worth two in the bush*.

This about *wraps it up*. It is time for me to *skedaddle*. Although I am not there with you, be assured that I am *tossing down* a few in your honor. Have a wonderfully *superduper* day, week, month, and year. May there be many more in your future.

Be assured that I really mean this, too. *I am not just whistling in the dark.*

Chasing Birthdays

Not too long ago, I spent five days deep in the hills of southern Appalachia, far from cell phones or signals; no television, no newspapers, no Wi-Fi, plenty of downtime, and few cares in the world. The only radio signal I could pick up was a 1932 broadcast of the Grand Ole Opry. The breeze blowing across my brow was trying to chase the beads of sweat away and was failing miserably. So there I sat on the cabin porch, wondering if someone would come by and hand me the jug or whether I would have to get up and retrieve it. I finally got up and grabbed it myself. The first (and the second) swig reminded me of an old girlfriend from years past who lived just up the holler...*the taste was hot and steamy.* It was sure good...at least as best as I can remember. But enough about me. Let me tell you about what happened this weekend up in them there mountains:

After hearing this prolonged noise of something thrashing through the woods, here comes this older looking man, maybe around my age, running through the clearing, and then he was gone before I could even wave. He was obviously very winded like he had been running for a long time. He was nude from the waist up and closer to dead than alive. And danged if he didn't look like a guy I used to know named Tony. It wasn't five minutes later that a second old guy, this one wearing a suit, came running in the same direction, maybe like he was chasing somebody. He had a briefcase in one hand and a shredded rag of some sort in the other. Once I figured out what the rag was, I knew this was a lawyer. Best as I can figure, he already had taken the shirt off of the first guy's back and appeared like he was going for more.

About that time, Ma stepped out onto the porch and saw what was happening. She said "No, that ain't no real lawyer. To be a lawyer you have to pass the bar and he ain't fast enough to pass them big old black bars we have around here." Since nobody else wears suits, in the Brushy, Big Walker, or Round Mountain area, we finally decided that he must be a parson. And that reminded me of one of the first Parsons I ever met, way back in the fifties...can't remember his last name but I think his first name was Tom.

Well, to make a long story short, the first guy was not chasing the second. They were both running from the same thing. It appears that the meanest, most mysterious, and unforgiving old codger in the hills had tried to ambush them a day or two ago. We locals call this unsavory old character Father Time. Every time the Father catches someone, he adds another year to their age. And for those who move too slow, he will eventually catch them enough times that they get so old they die.

So to whoever those old men were that I saw that day and each of you who are reading this here chronicle, all I can say is: "Boys and girls, he ain't caught you enough times just yet, so my best advice to you is, enjoy the moment and just keep on running!!!"

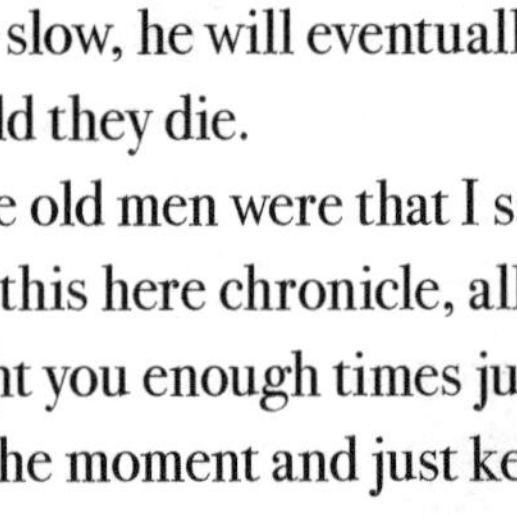

Message to a California Girl

During my lifetime I have corresponded with a wide range of folks from both the U.S. and abroad, from both the present and the past. While recently going through their letters, I found that many of them had something in common. They all had some type of association with Mill Valley, California. This little town of 14,000 population or so certainly attracted a lot of interest. For instance, did you know:

Musicians Janis Joplin, Huey Lewis, Jerry Garcia, and Bonnie Raitt lived there at one time. Carlos Santana lived nearby. John Lennon and Yoko Ono liked to summer there. This was the one place that they felt creative vibes radiating from the surroundings. They once told me the radiation was so strong that they almost felt like they were in Oak Ridge, Tennessee. Numerous authors dwelled in your little town at one time or another including Jack London who wrote *Call of the Wild.* (I often wondered if you were the inspiration for this title but never asked him.). When Jack Finney wrote *The Body Snatchers*, he struggled to come up with a title until he thought of you. I would have liked to have pursued that conversation with him further, but never got the chance.

One of my favorite people, fictional character B. J. Hunnicutt from the TV series *M*A*S*H* even told me that Mill Valley was his hometown. While he was happily married, he swore me to secrecy when he told me he chose Mill Valley for a hometown to be closer to you. And do you remember the movie *American Graffiti*? The sock hop scene was filmed in the high school gym. The director was, I think, inspired by my stories of your wild dancing in the Oak Ridge High School gym on numerous occasions.

Bottom line is, California girl, you in some little way must have been as much of an inspiration to them as you have been to so many of us back here in your old hometown. Some people think I exaggerate when I write of famous people I know or have been associated with over the years but rest assured I would not have known all this information if those celebrities had not personally told me. They, like me, miss your continuing presence in their lives. May every hug and kiss you get this day from your Marin County friends also represent the feelings of your friends from the great State of Tennessee, Oak Ridge Chapter.

Birthday Traditions

Have you ever wondered just when and how birthday celebrations began? Well, I am going to tell you.

The Bible makes reference to a Pharaoh's birthday back around 3000 B.C. This is the first known recorded mention of a birthdate being formally recognized. Shortly after that, famous Romans and the Greek gods were being recognized each year on the presumed date of their birth. Then sometime later, but still in ancient history, the Romans started recognizing the birthdays of other than the famous or the gods. Now the common man was included. Around the 12th century–after hundreds of years of nagging, cold shoulders, and denial of a man's given rights in the bedroom–women were also granted annual recognition of their birthdays.

From there it just grew. At first, Christians considered celebrations of this type as a pagan ritual. However, with the birth of Jesus, Christians adopted a new philosophy and the annual anniversary of His birth became a religious holiday. And remember, Jesus received gifts on his birthday.

Early in the eighteenth century, some enterprising German bakers got a brilliant idea. They invented not the Hallmark card, but the birthday cake, complete with candles for each year of age. This was at the urging of the local candle makers whose businesses were suffering from the longer days and warm nights caused by global warming. It didn't take long before other merchants, not wanting to miss out on the economic windfall, suggested each birthday celebration should be accompanied by special gifts from each friend or family member, such as those the baby Jesus received from the Magi. They called these type of gifts birthday presents.

Things stayed pretty much the same for many, many decades until a special group of ladies changed the whole philosophy of how to celebrate a birthday. I actually had the opportunity to witness one of these new celebration practice sessions. Now, I do not know whether this is a pagan or religious ritual, but the new way of celebrating is this:

A select group of female Oak Ridge Class of 1959 graduates, along with their associate members, get together on the designee's birthday or at a convenient time in close proximity and in unison wrap their lips around unopened bottles of wine and suck the corks off on the count of three. They then, using teeth only (makes no difference whether false or real) tilt the bottles up and chug-a-lug the whole thing. If any one of them screws up and lets some wine run down her chin, they do it again.

Well, ladies, I know you will be repeating this ritual many times during the next year. It is my sincere desire to witness at least one of these events. I do not know what the fee is to attend one of these sessions but please find enclosed my blank check to cover the down payment on the price of admission.

Till then, suck it up, girls, on each birthday and celebrate like you are just practicing for many, many more.

Ramblings

Naming of the Oak Ridge Elementary Schools

During the Manhattan Project initiated at the onset of World War II, the secret government city of Oak Ridge, Tennessee, was built to house the scientists and workers sent there to help develop the atomic bomb. The government built several elementary schools to accommodate all the children of the many people flowing into the city. Scarboro was named after an existing community. The other schools were all named after the natural surroundings in the area.

Names of the schools included: Elm Grove, Woodland, Pine Valley, Cedar Hill, Willowbrook, Linden, Glenwood, and Highland View.

In discussing how each of the schools originally got its name, one of my friends commented that, not being associated with trees or woods, Highland View broke the mold. He was wrong. The true story is somewhat unbelievable, but I needed to set the record straight. That provoked the following response:

Now it can be told. Highland View did not break the mold but was very much a part of it. Mary McGregor, a petite redhead and young deputy administrative assistant (secretary) to the Manhattan Project's L. B. Johnson, was selected to name each of the Oak Ridge neighborhood school districts in 1943. Mr. Johnson and his design team were much too busy for such trivial matters.

Well, ol' Mary done her job well while working her way west across the city. Each school district was named after nature's most prominent display, usually trees, on or near the locale where the building was to be erected. She did well until trying to decide the name for the next to last district. Amongst the beauty of the deeply wooded hills and valleys of early Oak Ridge was one area where the hillside was barren except for the native grasses and daisies. There was no glen surrounded on three sides by woods. There was no elm grove nor pine valley close by from which to draw inspiration. Neither was there a cedar hill nor any kind of trickling brook with willow trees lining its banks. In fact, there were no woodlands at all. As Mary walked this latest site searching for the right name she suddenly stopped and marveled at the magnificent view of the Cumberland Mountains to the west and the distant Great Smoky Mountains to the east. The view from the knoll was truly awe-inspiring and was completely unimpeded by any kind of vegetation above knee high. The terrain reminded Mary of her beloved highlands just outside of Dublin, Ireland, where she spent her childhood. Thus, in keeping with the tradition of naming each site based on the natural beauty of the land, the school soon-to-be-built there gained its name of Highland View. But there is more to the story.

The last school district to be named was the one that came closest to actually breaking the mold. Mary had been having an affair with her married boss, Lynn Johnson. She secretly wanted to name the last school after him but puzzled how to do so without anyone becoming suspicious. After much contemplation, and with her ability to pull a few strings, she had Lynn order several small Linden trees from Colorado and planted them one night on the grounds of what was to become the Linden Elementary School. Well, Lynn was none too happy with what had taken place. He wasn't so much upset that she had named the school district after him but was furious that she had spelled his name wrong.

Mr. Johnson's job was so secret that nowhere in the recorded records of the Manhattan Project does it show that he even worked there. Most people outside of Texas had never even heard of him until two decades later when he became President. Mary went on to work for him in civilian life also, and right up until his death she continued to mistype his signature block on his correspondence as follows: Linden B. Johnson, President of the United States.

How do I know this story is true? A long-dead little birdie told me. It was a female of the species and tweeted with a southern drawl. I called her Lady Bird.

You Can't Make This Stuff Up

Some folks ask, "Jerry, how do you come up with all the stuff you write about?" The answer is, I don't. Life writes the stories, and sometimes I am just the bystander recording the events for posterity. Other times I am the victim and just write down what happened. This is one of those times.

Nice guy that I am, I invited one of our sister Class of 1959 friends along with her above-the-age-of-consent daughter to spend one Friday night with us since they would be in town for a University of Tennessee football game. I did not go behind Sharon's back but got her permission. All was innocent, and the original plan was for Sharon to be home and share in the pleasure of hosting these lovely young ladies. But sometimes things don't work out as planned.

Sharon planned to go to Epcot and Disney World for a week to be a willing participant in the annual International Food and Wine Festival. She left on Saturday with plans to return on the following Friday, the day our guests were to arrive. All went well until Thursday when the airline canceled Sharon's return flight due to the impending arrival of Hurricane Irma. So there she was, in Orlando, Florida, with no way to get home and me in Oak Ridge with the possibility of having to spend an unchaperoned night with two desirable ladies.

While Sharon and her traveling companion scrambled to find a rental car that didn't cost more than buying a new one, I scrambled to identify which bar and grill I would take my guests to for Happy Hour. And unlike Sharon, price for me was no object. Anyway, we were both successful. Sharon left Orlando on Friday morning on what would ultimately be a twenty-five-hour ordeal trying to get out of Florida and into Georgia and eventually Tennessee without starving, running out of gas, or falling asleep at the wheel since there were no vacant motel rooms for nine hundred miles.

Rather than sitting home worrying about my wife, I put on the brave face and, with my two companions, met some friends at Applebee's for an alcohol-laced therapy session and group vigil. We fretted and stewed about Sharon's woes and troubles until the bar ran out of wine and beer. Then we all went home to continue our meditations individually or in smaller groups.

So now here I was, home alone with two women and I admit, we had all been drinking enough to lower our inhibitions to some degree. To top it off, I had never slept with either guest before. And they could not remember ever having slept with me. So what was a guy to do? I did what every man in my position would have done. We sat around talking until late in the night then I suggested we all go to bed.

About this time, Sharon was in hour fifteen or sixteen of her adventure, and I phoned her to 1) see where she was and how she was doing and 2) see if there was a possibility that she might walk in on us in the middle of the night. Once I received assurances that she was having a gourmet meal at the Pilot Truck Stop somewhere in Georgia and that the Pilot folks had provided a parking space for her so she could catch a couple hours sleep in the car, I told her how much I loved her and missed her. Then I hung up. My guests and I then went to bed, all three of us.

Now, my house has three bedrooms on the main level, so I know what you are thinking: who slept in which rooms? While all three of us will attest to the fact that everything that night was perfectly innocent, I had previously vowed that what happened in Oak Ridge would stay in Oak Ridge so I cannot give you details. I will tell you, however, that it does not mean a thing that two bedrooms were in perfect order and one wasn't when Sharon got home the next day. Even Sharon will attest to the fact that in the twenty-fifth hour when she finally arrived home and walked into the house at 9:30 a.m., we were all up and fully dressed, and none of us had a look of guilt on our face.

That is my story, and I am sticking to it.

Today I face a real dilemma. Today is Sharon's birthday. If I go out and buy her those diamonds like I want to, she is going to think I must have a guilty conscience and will become suspicious of my innocence. And if I get her something cheap, she is going to think I spent all my money on those other women.

So, Sharon, it is time you understood something. You do not need another diamond. You already have a diamond in the rough, all it needs is a little polishing. And, by the way, since you were not here to enjoy our guests, do you have a problem if I invite them back for next weekend?

Special Recognition

As far as I know, they did not attend Oak Ridge High School, so we do not think of them very often. But they grew up with us. I can remember them being at the Center Theater in Jackson Square on many Saturday afternoons. I also remember seeing them a time or two at both the Ridge and Grove theaters. They turned 77 today, but if you were to see them again after all these years, you would recognize them instantly. They haven't changed very much. Jasper (who later changed his name) has the same gray and white hair he always had and evidently still has a way with the ladies. His two favorite girlfriends back in the day, Toots and Toodles Galore, are still vying for his affections. And Jinx (who also later changed his name) is still the mousey type that he always was. But somehow, in spite of his small, meek appearance, he still seems to always come out on top.

I wouldn't exactly call them clowns for they were prone to become quite violent at times, especially with each other. But even in their worst moments they still had that knack for making us laugh. Their humor, if you remember, was more slapstick than subtle. The more they fought and antagonized each other, the less sorry we felt for either one of them. In spite of their intense disagreements most of the time, one always felt that deep down they were the best of friends. I remember them showing up that memorable day back in the late fifties when my dad brought home our first television set. They were both there to celebrate the occasion as I watched my first television show in my own home. And I appreciated their presence in my life at that time. I only hope that at some time in the past you had the same experience with them.

Anyway, I thought we should take this time to recognize their contributions to our teenage years. Little did we know back then that they would go on to make several movies, many television shows, and win seven academy awards. Thanks to William Hanna and Joseph Barbera, they've had stellar and successful careers. Happy 77th birthday, Tom and Jerry. You guys have not done badly for a couple of cartoon characters.

Hole in One

I heard about your golf "accomplishment," and I am somewhat confused. Why did you do it and why can't you keep your mouth shut? I do not play golf, so for you and all those other golfers out there, please bear with me and excuse my ignorance, if any. But I must ask, what is so notable about a hole-in-one? I am very sorry that you had witnesses and I know, or at least hope, you are embarrassed to have the newspaper folks find out about it. I know you can do better. I played my last golf game fifty years ago and used seven strokes on my worst hole. All the others required anywhere from nine to twelve strokes each. That was the reason I quit the game...it was much too easy.

Can you imagine a football team or participant scoring only one point and bragging about it? Or a baseball team? Softball team? Bowler? Basketball player? Volleyball player? Wrestler? Track or field competitor? Pinball machine player? Well, you get the picture. If you ever want to be a real winner you have to outscore the other opponent. You can't tell me that your hole-in-one was just bad luck. The odds are much too great.

Which leads me to a sad conclusion: did you have money bet on the golf game? Did you throw that hole on purpose? If so, you have two choices: 1) since the newspapers have already got hold of the story and there are credible witnesses, blame it on your brother. Or 2) if the heat is off, and you have collected your ill-gotten wagers, split the proceeds with me, and this analysis of what really happened will never see the light of day.

No Way to Treat a Lady

I had this dream a few years ago...or perhaps it was a nightmare. Anyway, it seemed so real that it was downright depressing. Or perhaps a better word would be heartbreaking. Based on real events at the time here in the real world, it was one of those dreams where facts got mingled in with fiction, and everything got all jumbled up. At least I hope that is what happened. There were some real people in my dream, and I possibly saw them in a less than flattering way. My apologies if this occurred. I do not have access to the real facts so I can only describe what I saw in my restless, tossing and turning, slumbering, and confused state of mind. It went something like this:

There I was, like a cloud or a wisp of wind floating over the beautiful East Tennessee countryside. I glanced down and noticed something unusual happening there on The Hill overlooking the University of Tennessee campus. I moved down a little closer for a better view and was somewhat surprised to see that it was a funeral.

There on that hallowed ground was an open grave with several people milling around, most dressed in black. There was no casket in sight, but people were placing something in the grave. Peering closer, I recognized the crumbled up items as Lady Volunteer symbols or logos, whichever one wants to call them. The softball coach dropped one in the grave, followed by the volleyball coach, the track coach, the swim coach, etc. Finally, every coach of a UT women's team but one had completed the ritual. All looked sad, and I saw a tear or two. But the most striking thing I noticed from my lofty perch was the distorted mouths that were all tightly closed. Upon closer inspection, I noticed that they had been all sewn shut. I wondered why.

The lone exclusion was Holly Warwick. She was hiding behind the administration building, grasping her team's Lady Vol symbol tightly with both hands and carrying a loaded .45 automatic side-arm on her hip. She was silently daring anyone to try and take the logo from her. I also noticed in my dream that nobody tried. At least not up to that time. I got the distinct impression that during all those years as an assistant to Pat, Coach Warwick had been taught well.

Other images caught my eye. Two gentlemen in dark suits stood next to the grave leaning on shovels, ready to complete the burial process at the appropriate time. They looked suspiciously like Chancellor Cheek and a shoe executive from out in Oregon. A third gentlemen–could this be the Athletic Director?–was at the head of the grave site. I assume he was going to conduct last rites. He must have memorized the words because the papers he held in his hand had "Marketing Plan" printed on them. I thought he looked like a real ladies' man. You know, the type that maintains firm control and knows how to keep a lady in her place. And was that a threaded needle that I saw him stick in his pocket?

From a fashion standpoint, all three gentlemen looked sharp; tailored dark suits with orange ties and each had a "Power T" pin in the lapel…the male version of course. All wore orange sneakers made by the same shoe manufacturer. The funny thing about the footwear were the soles, the part they walked on. These were colored powder blue for some reason.

None of the three wore hats. The two University of Tennessee representatives wore earplugs. I understood why they needed them although the only other folks in attendance were board members. The board had been so quiet for so long that their silence was deafening. I could not tell whether the shoe guy was wearing anything in his ears because the grin on his face was so big it hid all his other features.

A temporary fence had been erected about a hundred yards away to protect the sanctity of the funeral. Crowded against this fence were more than 23,000 people with looks of disbelief, hurt, and anger on their faces. None had come to view the funeral because none had yet accepted the fact that the Lady Volunteer symbol or logo had expired. They fully believed there may yet be some life left in the ol' girl and had come simply to deliver a message. One of the crowd members, obviously some sort of leader, thrust a stack of papers through the fence opening. The school guards holding the crowd back refused to take the papers and simply pointed to the sign on the fence that said: THE UT ADMINISTRATION DOES NOT ALLOW PETITIONS OR COMMON SENSE TO INFLUENCE THEIR DECISION MAKING.

The crowd was composed of many past and present Tennessee athletes: women and men, alumni, fans, donors, retirees, and others who believe in fair play, equal rights, tradition, and respect. I did not personally see Pat Summitt or Joan Cronan in the crowd but did feel their presence even way up from where I was viewing the scene.

To be totally fair to my dream, I did spot one single counter-demonstrator at the site who was fully in support of the logo elimination. The mere fact that she was a university employee who wrote letters to the editor of the local newspaper on university equipment during work hours because she was ordered to do so if she valued her job had nothing to do with the position she had taken.

As my dream came to an end, the final thing I viewed was what a University of Tennessee spokesperson called malicious vandalism. I know who did it and why. I'll just call them Joe and Jill Fan. They did it in support of the 23,000 petition signers, the many hundreds who wrote the school and local newspapers, and the tens or hundreds of thousands of other Tennessee Volunteer supporters who support the Lady Volunteer traditions and uniqueness.

The Power T with imprinted corporate shoe logo headstone was clandestinely removed during the night by a person or persons unknown. It was replaced with a simple marker with an epitaph that stated:

Here Lies the Lady Volunteer Logo
Intentionally Allowed to Die June 30, 2015
No Way to Treat A Lady

Postscript: Thank goodness that not all dreams are real. Today the Lady Vols logo is alive and well for all women's sports at the university. Nothing like this could ever happen at our beloved University of Tennessee, could it?

It Wasn't My Fault

Yes, Sharon does have a few stitches. Yes, there are visible bruises. Yes, there is a fractured bone involved. And yes, she has left our home for what I assume is a temporary period. But don't believe everything you hear. It wasn't my fault. I'll try my best to explain what really happened.

Sharon had a trip planned to cross the ocean last Friday, to sail the Rhine River on one of those Viking river cruises with, allegedly, a few girlfriends. At the same time, I was planning a trip to Martinsburg, West Virginia, to attend a wedding. All was well until I moved my trip up a day. Last Thursday as I was leaving home, Sharon followed me out the door to my car. Why I don't know. Perhaps I had failed to kiss her goodbye, or perhaps it was because I canceled her Visa card before she left town. Makes no difference. Anyway, here is where things get a little hazy.

As I opened the door to get in my car, I heard this funny noise, like someone had possibly fallen behind me and hurt his or herself. Sure enough, my instincts were right. I turned around and there lay Sharon, three steps below the porch on the driveway. I am totally convinced that it was just an accident and she just missed a step. The rumors that she threw her right foot at my rear end and missed is just speculation on someone's part. That girl loves me too much to do something like that. And it is obvious that I could not have pushed her since I was in front of her.

Don't you just hate these types of vicious rumors?

I saw a little blood on the knee, one foot twisted in an awkward direction, and a lot of pain was on her face. Other than that, everything looked normal. I asked her if she thought she could get up and walk and she said "yes.". With this reassurance from her that she was ok, I helped her get to her feet, watched her return to the house, then, feeling good about how well I had demonstrated my husbandly concern, got in the car and headed North toward West Virginia.

Being the loving husband that I am, I stopped some five or six hours later and called Sharon to check on her and remind her that she might need to put some ice on the foot. It turns out that at that time she was sitting in the orthopedic doctor's office. Evidently, Sharon must have done something else to herself after I left for she was now in serious pain and couldn't walk very well. I was shocked to hear this since she had told me she was ok when I left the house. I almost asked her if I should return home but refrained from doing so as not to put her on the spot.

Anyway, all is now well. I made the wedding just fine, and for those of you who were worried about whether I would make it on time, I was right on schedule thanks to not having to return to Oak Ridge.

Friday morning, Sharon e-mailed me that she made enough of a miraculous recovery to get to the airport for her trip. Since then I have received a couple of other communications from her from various towns in Germany. She told me that thanks to her personal doctor and nurse that she hired to travel with her, she is now able to walk fine. She further informed me that I forgot to cancel her American Express card. She has shopped the last two days and has a few more to go and that, since she is such a good member, American Express will not charge extra for her exceeding the $10,000 limit.

Sharon is scheduled to return home this weekend, and I am very much looking forward to seeing her again. For any of you friends in the Oak Ridge area, I am supposed to pick her up at the Knoxville airport Saturday night and am a little short on cash. American Express has already notified me that they have executed a garnishment of my future retirement and Social Security checks. May I borrow your car or enough money for gasoline? And also, depending on the mood she is in, I might need a loan to cover the cost of hiring my own personal doctor. Thanks.

The Rest of the Story

Sometimes the evenings get a little too quiet. When that happens, I either watch television, drink a few brews, or sit around thinking. At the risk of boring you, here is what I was thinking about one evening while drinking those few brews because there was nothing on television worth watching. I was thinking about a story I heard a long time ago. I assume the story is true and I hope my somewhat unstable memory does not botch up the retelling too badly.

Are you old enough to remember a musical group from the 1950s and 1960s called The Drifters? Shortly after I graduated from high school back those many years ago, The Drifters, led by the great Ben E. King at the time, recorded a song titled "Save the Last Dance for Me.". This song, which I think was the Number One song in the nation for three or four weeks, was written by two guys named Doc Pomus and Mert Shuman. I'll not cite the lyrics here for copyright reasons but hope you will look the words up and maybe even listen to the song.

"Save the Last Dance for Me" is about a man who, on a very special occasion, finds himself at a dance with the love of his life. Dancing is not for him, so he tells her to go have fun, dance with all the guys. It's ok if they smile at you and put their arms around you. Just remember, at the end of the evening you are going home with me.

He further tells her in verse two to enjoy the music. Laugh and sing, girl, but do not give your heart to any of those guys you are dancing with. Remember who you will be going home with, darling. That last dance is mine.

In verse three he proclaims his eternal love for her and vows to never let her go. He again encourages her to dance with others but not to fall for any of their smooth talk. If any suggestions are made beyond just dancing, turn them down. His thinking is, "The last dance is mine, and I'll be the lucky one who takes you home."

Great song. Great era. Brings back great memories. But there is more to tell.

According to legend, Doc Pomus, the songwriter, wrote this song on his wedding day. Doc's wife-to-be was a Broadway actress and an accomplished dancer. The song reflected both Doc's love for his new wife and his perspective on how he felt at his wedding reception. For you see, Doc was unable to dance. He could not even stand without crutches. He was a polio victim and was confined to a wheelchair.

As Paul Harvey would say, "Now you know the rest of the story."

How Country Songs Get Written

You know, it's funny how an instant in time or a few flippant words can make such a significant impact on one's life. But that is what happened to He. I call him "He" and the other person in my story I'll just call "She" because names don't really matter. And if this little tale is fiction or fact is not really important either. I will tell you, however, that the described instant in time and few flippant words are true for I personally heard them spoken. The rest of what you are about to read comes from thoughts triggered by someone who loves words, loves life, and loves music.

Let's get one thing straight at the beginning. He is happily married and has been for many years. She is a strictly platonic friend and is, I think, lovingly involved with a special man in her life. He and She are, however, good friends and have known each other ever since their high school days. Back then they were mere acquaintances. In the last few years, they've gotten to know each other better and are now good friends whose paths cross fairly often.

He and She found themselves together at a gathering of friends recently. At some point during the evening, they had the opportunity to engage in a private conversation for just a moment or two. This was the instant in time that I mentioned earlier. He thought of how cute and friendly she was in high school (and of course still is) and jokingly leaned over and asked her, "If things were different and we both suddenly found ourselves uncommitted or unattached, would I have a chance with you?"

Next came the few spoken words alluded to earlier that changed his life. Her answer, while really a non-answer, was both confusing to him yet very definitive. She simply said, "There are two things I have never liked, and one of them is white socks."

He was somewhat taken back by her response and in a confused manner slowly looked down at the floor. The only thing he saw was his bright freshly washed white socks which he put on especially for the afternoon gathering. I probably don't need to tell you they had replaced the black socks that he initially put on when he got up that morning.

But He was unruffled and never showed his confusion with her answer. He simply asked her, "What is the second thing you never liked? Her response was "I can't remember.". He wondered out loud if it was possibly "Rednecks" and while She was noncommittal, She did not deny the possibility. Needless to say, He had lived in Tennessee most of his life and proudly considered himself to be an East Tennessee Redneck in good standing.

This was strike one and probably strike two, so He was glad She had not mentioned a third thing She did not like. He did not ask her any more questions for He did not want to hear her next answer. Some things are better left unsaid.

After mulling over their conversation for a couple of days, He was perplexed by the thought that his choice of sock colors and his natural heritage had such a profound influence on what another possibly thought of him, even if the comment was offered in a good-natured and kidding sort of way. What was a guy in this situation to do?

What do all good Rednecks from East Tennessee that drink beer and own a pickup truck do when they have been spurned by a woman? He picked up his pen and paper, grabbed a six pack of cold beer–it could have been Pabst Blue Ribbon–jumped in his truck, and drove out to the old railroad trestle crossing the Clinch River. He was down to two choices: jump in and end it all or drink a few beers and write a country song.

The choice was easy. Ol' George had his "He Stopped Loving Her Today" Willie has his "Blue Eyes Crying in the Rain;" and Hank had his "I'm So Lonesome I Could Cry." Well, ol' He did not have a broken heart from She's lack of interest in him, but he pretended he did. After all, great classic country music involves broken hearts as well as hard drinking, pickup trucks, jukeboxes. Mamas, and other classic ingredients. Well, He had them all. At least He was able to pretend he did. The hard drinking, pickup truck, and Mama were all there. Mama was gone but was still present in many ways. His heart was not broken right now but had been many times in his younger days. And while jukeboxes are no longer found in very many places, the memories of that jukebox in his favorite bar during his military service many years ago still brings a tear to his eye whenever He thinks about all the cheap beer he drank and the many nickels he spent playing those sad songs that in some unexplainable way made him feel better rather than worse as he contemplated his life's woes, sorrows, heartbreak, and home. (Yes, I know that is a long sentence and one that would be difficult to diagram or even justify to our high school English teachers, but this is not an English class essay. This is a real story about a real man living a real life in turmoil.)

He poured his heart into the lyrics of his song. He had either lived the heartache that motivated him or at least imagined he did. Perhaps if He captured the words to each verse in a particularly touching and poignant manner, She's biased against white socks would be lessened. And if the song moved her enough, perhaps She would close her eyes and even forget just how red He's neck really was.

He wrote with passion. He wrote with conviction. He ran out of beer and had to go buy some more (was it Miller High Life this time?) just to maintain the mood that was fueling his creative juices. And the final product would do Nashville proud.

Thank you, She. Your offhand comments to He that day inspired a work of country artistry so impressive that if Handel were still alive and could hear it, he would rewrite his "Messiah" to have more of a country twang.

I ran into He the other day, and he relayed most of this little story to me. He knew he had a classic tune that would one day be recognized as one of the great ones, ranking right up there with Hank and Willie's finest. I actually overheard him sing his song, and I have to agree. Once He learns to play the guitar and sing on key, it will be even better. I begged him to allow me to share the lyrics with you but he refused. He did allow me to share the title: "*Red Neck, White Socks, and the Blues.*" I hope you get to hear it one day.

His final words to me struck a chord even in my own life. He said, "Jerry, do you know the reason this song was so personal and so easy to write? It is because, just like your Sharon, every word She speaks is music to my ears".

So, gals and guys, my advice to you is to listen more closely to that special man (or two) or woman (or two) in your life and simply write down whatever feelings their words invoke in your heart.

That, my friends, is how great country songs get written.

Beware of Derby Parties

Well, it happened again. You grow up with friends, think you know them, and–for those who live in and around the Oak Ridge-Knoxville, Tennessee, area–even look forward to socializing with them every now and then. Tonight was one of those nights. The occasion was a so-called Derby party. The horse whisperer was there from Middle Tennessee with some young trophy chick passing through town on her way to Warrington, Virginia. The Knight of Avalon hosted the party along with his fair maiden from Oak Ridge. The Captain and his cabin girl sailed in from Ten Mile, Tennessee. Also waltzing in was the Dancing King from our last class reunion escorted by the Cat Lady; and no, she is not the one from the Batman comics. And finally, the lone other attendee, other than yours truly and bride, was a ghostly figure from the 1500s, looking as young as she did when the Lost Colony first got lost. Although she did not know where she was, she claimed the entire Outer Banks population of North Carolina was out looking for her.

One would think with friends like this a good time was waiting. Friends, don't believe it. If you are ever invited to party with them, all I can say is grab your billfold or purse with both hands and run as fast as you can. I learned this the hard way.

Upon arriving at the castle gate, I was accosted by a doorman who demanded a *statement of net worth* before allowing our entrance. After convincing him that I was a poor old retiree struggling on a fixed income, Sharon and I were allowed to proceed; but only after I produced my checkbook, which showed a balance of twenty-two dollars. So far, so good. The hospitality inside was something to behold. The bourbon balls were delicious. The food was plentiful but mostly alcohol-free. The rest of the place was alcohol full. The beer, wine, and whiskey flowed as freely as the east fork of Poplar Creek flowing out of the Y-12 National Security Complex. And there was a demon of a drink called a *Mount Juliet*. I don't know whether it was the Middle Tennessee version of a mint julep or a real mint julep mispronounced by a less-than-sober amateur bartender. Bottom line, I thought I was having a good time. They kept plying me with drinks and, not wanting to hurt anyone's feelings, I kept drinking them. Little did I know there was an ulterior motive taking place.

Well, I'm not going to bore you with details. Suffice to say, they loosened my inhibitions and enticed me to play their stupid little game of "place a bet on a horse and win big bucks for first, second, third, or last place.". They juggled the rules and the amount one could bet just right. It cost Sharon and me exactly twenty bucks to bet on four horses and two more for guessing which one would finish last. That took care of my twenty-two dollars and left me with thirty-seven cents in my pocket, and darned if someone didn't pickpocket that! What hurt the most is Sharon was in on it. She claimed she was my date and made me pay the whole amount.

Guess what? I lost. I know you're shocked. So was I. I don't know how they fixed that race but they did. And lied about it with a straight face. And afterward claimed they felt sorry for me. And refused to loan me gas money to get home. The only salvation was that I cried in my beer so much that I got an extra two glasses to drink before I was cut off. I got even with one of them, though. I siphoned gas out of somebody's car shortly after they kicked me out of the house.

So, friends, I leave you with this final thought. If you ever get invited to a party of this type...Go! Everyone tells me that in spite of the adversities I suffered, I had a great time. And because I know them, I believed them. And we all agreed that there was only one thing missing. You.

Out of This World Advice

You Earth people are totally crazy. You fear radiation yet use a far more dangerous substance without any consideration as to the damage it is doing. With tongue firmly inside cheek and mouth closed to protect from the humidity in your atmosphere, I offer the following thoughts for your consideration.

I am from Oak Ridge, Htrae. Htrae is a planet very similar to earth except nuclear applications have been part of our lives for many generations. We enjoy the many benefits and have learned to control the hazards to such an extent that we now take radiation almost for granted. We have heard all your arguments relative to the dangers and laugh at your ignorance. But you have something that is different–and that we have recently discovered–and it scares the heck out of me.

We never knew what water was until a few decades ago when it was developed in one of our government laboratories. Our world became excited as the benefits were quickly recognized. Water could replace milk, juices, and other natural fluids as nourishment for our bodies. It had the ability to extinguish fire. It had cleansing properties to remove dirt from many things. It was a great accelerant for growing our crops and plants when sprinkled on regularly and in moderation. For some applications, it could be used as a lubricant to reduce friction. It has shown great promise as a coolant for industrial uses. Other beneficial uses are being discovered every day. But at what cost?

Wake up, Earthlings. Don't be blinded by your politicians and special interest groups. Don't let apathy rob your children and grandchildren of a better, safer life. Don't let your continued love affair with water rob you of all common sense relative to the dangers of this substance. Do not jeopardize your entire planet and your very existence. Our researchers on Htrea have identified and documented many of the hazards that the presence of water presents and more are being identified every day. Here are a few examples:

1. Excessive water causes erosion, robbing the soil of nutrients required for growing food and at the same time creating unsafe walking and driving conditions. People are already starving on many parts of your planet due to the lack of fertile ground and are dying in vehicle wrecks due to uneven terrain. Trips and falls are quite common due to this condition. Your Grand Canyon represents a glaring example of erosion and should serve as a warning and deterrent. It is only a matter of time until Los Angeles or perhaps Oliver Springs suffers a similar fate.
2. Water weakens or destroys many materials, such as paper, cardboard, unprotected wooden products, etc. Whether it can do the same to human skin is as yet undetermined. Some of our scientists think it might also cause hair loss. It is my understanding that many earthlings routinely rub soap and water on their hair. Have any of your people noticed thinning hair or perhaps balding as they age?

3. Water will shrink or destroy certain materials such as clothing, salt, sugar, Kleenex, etc. This is based on relatively short-term observations. The long-term effects and other materials at risk are still unknown at this time.
4. Water evaporates and disappears when exposed to excessive heat. Where does it go and what happens to it? There is some evidence that evaporated water is dispensed into the upper atmosphere, where under certain natural conditions it will fall back to the ground as a liquid in uncontrollable amounts. So far there is no known way to control the locations into which it will fall. Water drops falling from the sky appear to be relatively harmless, but the danger lurks in the changes it undertakes when falling through a below-freezing atmosphere. It is estimated that frozen water drops can range in size from a dime to maybe as large as a baseball. Just imagine what damage or injury could occur from being hit by such missiles.
5. Even if confined to Earth, water becomes virtually useless in cold weather, turning into a semi-solid slush or becoming a solid. While the solids can be used in small amounts to cool food or beverages, is the risk worth it? In our laboratory tests, water has rendered such diverse items as potato chips and Twinkies as essentially tasteless. Also, every liquid into which it comes in contact is diluted and weakened. Without exception the more water you add, the weaker the liquids and greater the adverse effects. Why do your medical personnel often recommend taking medicine with water? Does this not lessen the effect of the prescribed dosage?
6. Vehicles can become uncontrollable when driven on water. Slushy or frozen water compounds the problem. How many

Earth people die each year from water-related and winter driving accidents? You turn a blind eye to the real problem and continually blame these tragedies on weather conditions, speed, or driver error.

7. Water can cause even the finest machinery and metals to oxidize and become corroded. If allowed to continue for any length of time, the metal products become useless, and the only remedy is to replace them at great cost. Even worse is the safety factor. The failure of an airplane engine from water-based corrosion during flight can have fatal results for all who are on board. On the other hand, sometimes failure of a metal device can be a good thing from a moral or safety standpoint. How many more children in Chicago would be alive today if those metal firearms used by gang bangers failed from rust or oxidation?
8. Water is a conductor of electricity. Free-flowing water carrying electricity is a proven killer of plants, animals, and humans.
9. Unless maintained in its purest form, water will become toxic and germ-laden, spreading disease and illness to those who come in contact. Intake of this type of water into the body can often be deadly. Have you ever heard the phrase when visiting certain places, "Don't drink the water?" There are good reasons for warnings of this type. Over a million deaths on your planet last year were attributed to diseases spread by contaminated water.
10. Laboratory tests have shown that as little as a teaspoon of water trapped in the lungs can kill a person. Just think what a water-filled balloon could do if a terrorist tossed one into a crowd of people with their mouths open when the balloon

> burst. This would be compounded a thousand-fold if one were to fill a weather balloon with water and drop it on one of your heavily populated cities.

In their misguided attempts to control water, the people on Earth have created massive lakes and dams that allow deep pools of water to form. And we suspect the evaporation process and ultimate return to earth in the form of rainfall has created what you call the oceans, which keep growing every year. How long will it be until the Earth is fully covered and all land-based life ceases to exist? Just this past year on Earth more than 360,000 people drowned and at least that many more had to be saved by others from a similar fate. Every single one of these deaths could have been avoided if people just simply avoided all contact with water.

Think of all the purification systems in existence in all the towns and cities, all the dams, all the canals, all the viaducts, all the piping systems used to safely move water to individual houses and businesses. Think of the cost of water protection systems, such as umbrellas, raincoats, hats, etc. Think of the cost of all the safety containers and instruments, e.g., cups, glasses, buckets, tanks, storm drains, mops, sponges, etc. that are required for the safe handling of water. These and the other required water controls literally cost billions and billions of dollars every year. I dare speculate that if all this water could be eliminated there would be enough wealth to eliminate poverty from the entire earth.

I could go on and on but hope this is enough for you to get my message. As I leave you, I do not want to be accused of using irrational scare tactics to make my case. I have tried to present the facts as we have identified them to date based on unbiased examination and observation. Weigh this information for what it's worth and then make up your own mind. In the meantime, I will return to my own planet, where the dangers of your alien world do not exist. Now that I think about it, I don't think we had a single radiation-related death last year. And the danger of a reactor meltdown is less than that of one of your TVA dams breaking or one of your politicians telling the truth. In fact, I just today learned that your TVA's Boone Dam is leaking and will require an estimated 450 million dollars to repair. TVA failed to make public how many lives downstream from the dam are at risk. When we have a reactor leak, we just shut it down. How do you shut down a leaking dam?

Old habits die hard, so I do not expect my warnings to be heeded. If you persist in not changing your ways, I leave you with this one last request: when taking a shower, please remember to keep your mouth closed. And if you have children, you might consider taping their mouths shut during the cleansing process. And for heaven's sake, teach them not to swallow so they do not accidentally get any water in their mouths. These children are the future. They deserve to be as water-free as possible.

Trouble at the Old Folks Hangout

Chapter 1–The Incident

The call came in sometime after dark. I'm not sure exactly what time because I couldn't find my glasses. A body had been found at the PussyCat Den, a seedy little juke joint out on River Road that had been a trouble spot for decades. Years ago, before being relocated to its current site, it was a high school hangout for those pathetic teenagers who either couldn't get a date on Friday night or did not have enough money to buy a quart of beer at the Midtown Market. They probably did not have a very good quality fake driver license, anyway. People had died at the Pussycat Den before, but mostly of old age. This may be the first homicide.

My name is Starr...Jackie Starr. I never liked the name Jackie, so I asked my friends to call me "Super.". Time to saddle up and go to work. And for those who are not familiar with my town, there are twenty-seven thousand stories in the Secret City. This is just one of them.

Being healthy for my age, but neither wealthy nor wise, I drive a city-furnished 1956 Ford Fairlane, plain black with a working spotlight. I call my car Jane. She is equipped with a fairly modern 2006 Garmin three-inch dash-mounted GPS unit to help me recall my way around town. Our fine city, being wealthier and wiser than me, denied my request for a new police cruiser to cover the cost overruns on the new urinal installed in the public men's restroom out near the marina.

Well, Ol' Jane fired right up, and I found my way to the Den in near record time. I would have been even faster if that dadgum siren worked. The hand crank handle broke off last week, and I never got it replaced. Taking the wrong turn out of the parking lot didn't help my response time either.

Many of the PussyCat regulars were still hanging around when I arrived, some in wheelchairs or on walkers, some on canes, and all with a drink in their hands. Some of them had not even heard there was a problem. Faulty hearing aids, I guess. I was confused for an instant, thinking I was at the Snow White Nursing Home instead of the Den. There was a Whole Lot of Shakin' Going On, and it wasn't caused by Jerry Lee Lewis. These people were old! They had obviously been affected with Age. This is a cruel disease for which there is no known cure. Some looked like they'd had it for years.

Anyway, as I entered the joint that 1950s-era jukebox was talking to me. An old soul singer named Jerry Butler was telling the world that *"He don't love you like I love you..."** Jerry went straight to the heart. He was singing about Betty Lou Buxom and me! I had loved her more than anyone else did for almost fifty-five years, but I didn't want the whole city to know it, especially her husband...or ex-husbands...or my wife. We went this long without getting caught, and I don't need this kind of trouble now.

Sorry, but I got sidetracked for a minute.

After emptying seven shells from my Ruger 9mm into that stupid jukebox, I approached the prone, inert, downright ugly body still lying on the floor. There was little blood, but there was a huge knot, about the size of a size ten boot, and associated purple bruising on the side of the head just above the left ear. Some of the not-yet-evaporated liquid underneath the body was obviously urine that, to my highly trained sensory skills, originated from either Miller High Life or vintage Falstaff. We don't need a coroner or evidence team on this one. The guy, without doubt, suffered a fatal blow to the head either before, during, or right after death. He had been drinking prior to death, and the diamond earring was fake.

I recognized the body. Steve Double was his name. He had once been my best friend back in high school until I found out he French-kissed my first real girlfriend three weeks before I did. At least his brother and some other guys waited until I first had a shot at her. As for Steve, in his current condition, I didn't know whether to kick the kissing son of a donkey in the head or interview some of the regulars still hanging around to see what they witnessed or knew.

I did what any good cop would do in a similar situation: never pass up a chance for a free beer. I walked behind the bar to retrieve a mug. Big mistake. There was another body lying on the floor. The first glance told me everything I needed to know. It was Mark Double. This guy was marginally better looking than his younger brother, and the only difference according to the visible evidence was that he had been drinking a quart bottle of Colt 45, probably from that Midtown grocery store down the road. An early vow of his was ringing in my ears: "I resolve to stand (or fall) by my brother…I will drink as much as he does.".

Thank goodness he and his brother didn't drink everything. I reached over the body and grabbed me a beer. It looked like we had a case of Double trouble.

Chapter 2–The Physical Evidence

I examined Mark's body closely. Again, there was no need for a coroner. Same symptoms as his brother and same conclusion: knot on the head, purple bruising, deader than a doornail and another guy that kissed my high school girlfriend. I somehow refrained from kicking this second son of a donkey in the head, too.

Now, let us look at the physical evidence as we try to determine who is responsible for this wanton taking of lives. I checked the fingerprints on the beer bottles that both corpses still grasped in their hands. Steve Double's prints were a perfect match for those found on his beer bottle. Mark Double's prints were a perfect match for the prints found on his beer bottle.

For both deceased, the knots on the heads were compared not only to those of a size ten boot, which was probably a coincidence, but also to those portions of the floor with which they came into contact. Again, the evidence is overwhelming that both heads hit the floor. From measuring their height and weight relative to the density of the floor at the point of collision, it is evident that the size of the bruising is consistent with the anticipated volume of blood that would have rushed to that point of the body during a blow of this type.

A third point of evidence indicates that in life the Doubles had looked similar, weighed about the same amount, lived similar lives, and probably even had the same parents. It is assumed that they might have been good looking at one time, before their lifestyles caught up with them. One would have thought they were twins except one of them was a few minutes older than the other.

While not conclusive, they each delivered *The Oak Ridger* newspaper during their youth. At this time, there is no evidence that this coincidence contributed in any way to their deaths.

And finally, while I am neither wealthy nor wise, I am thorough. We examined all the quarters that had been deposited into the jukebox. One quarter came up positive for Steve's fingerprint and another quarter contained a partial thumbprint that tested as 99 percent positive as that of Mark's. This is further proof that Mark's finger was not stuck up his rear end at the time of death. At least not his left thumb.

Further analysis indicated that both individuals had at some time during the evening played jukebox selection F23, perhaps even multiple times. This particular selection just happened to be titled "He Don't Love You (Like I Love You)" by Jerry Butler. This was a very significant finding in the ultimate solution and closing of this case.

Chapter 3–The Interviews

The interviews were the most frustrating part of trying to solve this case. While I had no problem asking the right questions of the interviewees (because I had written the questions down beforehand), I had a very difficult time extracting answers. There were two problems: 1) most of those knowledgeable about the case had a serious memory problem, and 2) I forget what the other problem was.

Because of widespread memory lapses, most interviews were very short. But I was still able to obtain information that contributed heavily to the ultimate solution to this case. A brief summary of each interview is as follows:

1. Deedee Dancer.–*I don't remember anything. I was busy slow dancing to that song that kept playing on the juke-*

box. After that, I went upstairs and made out with what-is-his-name just like in the old days.

2. Glory Halleluiah: *I was busy enjoying the day while listening to the jukebox while reading the newspaper and exercising my left arm. I heard a couple of thuds but did not look up to see what was happening.*
3. Keith V. Cleaner: *While some may say I was playing bocci while jogging in place on one leg due to a bad knee caused by a run-in with a baseball bat during my younger days, do not necessarily believe them. I am a lawyer and know my rights. I plead the Fifth. No, wait. I think I drank the fifth. No wait, I ...By the way, what was that song playing on the jukebox?*
4. Annie Jo Sleepover: *I remember nothing except the music and the great time I had sampling all the new wines in stock. They were lip-licking good. If you like good wine, you can lick my lips anytime.*
5. Bill Singer: *I witnessed both gentlemen's last moments of life. I am the house entertainer, and I had just finished my last set. I really didn't think my rendition of "Blue Eyes Crying in The Rain" was that bad, but they pulled the plug on my guitar, took two quarters out of my tip jar, and ran toward the jukebox. It wasn't long after that that they both seemed so drunk that they couldn't stand up. Next thing I knew, they were both on the floor, each with a tear in his eye. And be sure to mention in your report that I have a better memory than most of the other folks in here.*
6. Larry Branston: *I cannot say anything negative about my beloved Tennessee Vols or any of my friends here at the PussyCat Den except that I didn't like the Double broth-*

ers' reaction to that song on the jukebox. The song bothered me, too, but not enough to kill myself. Or anyone else. Other than that, I know nothing. Dang, it's so much responsibility being perfect.

7. Jack O. Lantern: *I didn't see anything, I was busy multi-tasking. Trying to read, play table tennis, and beat a lawyer at bocci without getting sued kept me pretty well occupied. I did see both victims on the floor but didn't think anything was unusual. That looked like their natural position to me.*
8. J. L. Rhymer: *I was sitting over in the corner listening to my favorite Jerry Butler song while trying to dislodge my tongue from my cheek. Later, I spent some time cleaning my boots. I'll miss those guys. I don't mean to reminisce at a time like this, but do you remember when you, Steve, Mark, and I shared the same girlfriend a long time ago? Sure wish I'd been first.*
9. Kate Steward: *What the heck do you think I could see from three thousand feet overhead in a balloon filled with hot air? That is where I was after smoking my newest pain medicine. I haven't been that high since I was a stewardess smoking toke while Captain Mac tried to have his way with me. He later claimed I passed my initiation into the club. I know nothing about what took place here since I arrived just five minutes before you did. Thank you for shutting down that darn jukebox. That song brings back bad memories.*
10. Relma Walker: *Don't ask me, I know nothing. I've had about all I can take in this stuffy place, I need to take a hike to the Top of Ol' Smoky. I do not mind walking that*

far for clean air, but I ain't walking fifteen miles or more for a Camel.

11. Tony Racer: *I saw nothing. I was busy counting all my surgery scars. I heard no jukebox music, spent most of the evening griping about losing ten bucks in some stupid PussyCat Den trivia contest that was fixed from the start and was thinking about my sex marathon. Oops, I meant next marathon. Well. An old guy can dream, can't he?*
12. Jim Boatman, Captain USCG: *Don't ask me, man. I was sitting near the dock of the bay. I didn't even leave the boat until Annie Jo and Kate called me and told me the "coast" was clear. I didn't understand their terminology. We call it "shore" here in Tennessee. And since my wife stayed home tonight, I shore had a lot of fun with those two gals.*
13. Will Shipman: *I went out to the kitchen to fix a submarine sandwich and missed everything. I had a sinking feeling it was going to be a bad evening.*
14. Tom Lawyer: *Super, you know better than to ask me any questions. I expect to be involved in the case as legal counsel for the Den and have to invoke attorney/client privilege.* Note to file: this guy's testimony would be worthless anyway. After all, who is going to believe a lawyer?
15. Mary Howard: *Oh dear. My husband and I just flew in from Texas and were supposed to spend the night at the Double's house. What will we do now? Does this place stay open all night? And, by the way, do you remember the name of that song playing on the jukebox?*

Chapter 4–Conclusion

Well, it was time to wrap up this case. The evidence was in, the interviews conducted. Follow-up investigation after the interviews revealed no new information of significance. The fact that J. L. wore size ten boots on the night in question was ultimately determined to be a nonfactor. Neither was the fact that I also wear size ten shoes. We are both too old and feeble to kick up our heels hard enough to hurt anyone.

While space prevents me from documenting everything I learned in this investigation, additional information is well known. Let's look at what we have learned so far:

Routine background checks revealed that Steve Double aspired to a late-life career in politics and had even filed in his home district to run for a seat in the U. S. House of Representatives. Mark Double, because he hated politicians, had vowed to stop Steve by all means possible. Both were known to be heavy drinkers and shallow thinkers. Neither had bothered to consult with an attorney about their aspirations. Of course, any good lawyer worth his or her salt would have lied to them anyway.

The PussyCat Den was and is a hangout for a bunch of old coots that are too old to even remember their age. In Oak Ridge, Tennessee, PussyCats grow up to be Wildcats, so don't make them mad. And the Den is not always located on River Road. It is wherever this cult-like group chooses to gather. They went to school together and never got over it. They live in both the present and in the past and play late-50s and early-60s music. They keep in regular contact through email and think it is more important to meet face-to-face occasionally rather than use Facebook or Twitter. While they can call themselves old, they are younger than most folks I know. They care for each other and maintain close contact after six decades. They include their spouses and significant others in their activities, except when it is more convenient to not do so. They laugh together, cry together, celebrate together, mourn together and, when needed, pray together. Do they go around killing each other? I think not. They grew up in an age of innocence and never changed. They are a pleasure to be around and are true friends. I am blessed to be a part of them.

After examining all the evidence, I have drawn only one conclusion. Read this report, examine the facts, and read between the lines. While the physical evidence might point in one or more directions, there is one constant that cannot be avoided: the music. It takes control. It evokes emotions that touch the soul. It brings smiles, laughter, tears, and a gamut of other emotions that words cannot describe. Can it even bring murder? Possibly.

My conclusion is: some call him The Ice Man, some call him Jerry. I call him one of the greatest singers of our generation. He just kills every song he sings!

The Butler did it.

Respectfully submitted this ninth day of January 2014,

Jackie Starr

Jackie "Super" Starr, Lead Investigator

Secret City Police Department

Epilogue

Deep in the bowels of the Secret City Medical Center, Dr. Bommy Towers, pathologist and morgue administrator was apologizing to the two strangers in his presence. "Sorry fellows, everyone thought you were both dead. I'm sure glad I heard the two of you burp in unison before taking that first autopsy cut. Now that you have finally come out of those alcohol-induced comas, I'll call you a cab".

Upon arrival, the cab driver asked his fares, "Where to, gentlemen?" With a slight smile on his face, the younger one replied, "PussyCat Den. I need a drink after the night I've had."

The End

*From "He Don't Love You (Like I Love You)," Curtis Mayfield, Calvin Carter, Jerry Butler. Also titled "He Will Break Your Heart."

Measuring Managers and Organizations

During my five decades of working for many good and not-so-good bosses and superiors, I formed my own philosophy for measuring the effectiveness of supervisors, managers, and organizations. If you are in the workforce as a leader or one aspiring to a leadership position, I provide this summary for your consideration.

Is your organization capable? Is it respected by others? How do you measure its value (and values)? Look at the people around you. And remember, what you see may be a reflection of yourself. Learn from it.

So, how do you know when you are good? You are good when:

- You assign a task and know it will get done.
- Your people never "bad-mouth" their own group or organization.
- You include your staff in the decision-making process.
- Your staff supports decisions after they are made.
- Every internal complaint about the way things are done is accompanied by a suggestion or recommendation for how to improve.
- You listen to your people and they listen to you.

- Performance evaluations are based on performance, not pedigree.
- You give your word and it is believed.
- No one says, “That is not my job.”
- Your people know you will support them.
- The group functions just as efficiently in your absence.
- More people want to get into your organization than want to get out.
- You recognize that mistake-free people do very little work.
- Your people do not make the same mistake twice.
- You have an open-door policy, and no one visits.

The Bear Facts

So there I was, out mowing grass in the meadow of our little mountain hideaway in southwestern Virginia. This place is unoccupied most of the year. It was my son's turn to mow, and my grandson and I had met him there just to enjoy a quiet, peaceful weekend in the mountains. Why I volunteered to drive 240 miles just to help him mow and weed eat those three or four acres, I'll never know. But I will remember this trip.

I took my riding mower to Virginia, and we also have another one located at the cabin. I was on one mower, my son was on the other, and my grandson was using the weed-eater. Everything was uneventful most of the afternoon. I was mowing the area near our cabin and passed under this nearby tree at the edge of the meadow numerous times. Finally, I was ready for a break; parked the mower and headed for the house which was about 15 to 20 yards away.

Just as I reached the front porch for the sole purpose of retrieving a cold beer from the cooler, my grandson came running while shouting, "Bear, Bear!" Now my grandson is known to exaggerate, but this time he was right. A bear was in the process of descending from the tree which was originally thirty yards away but now looked to be twenty-five yards closer. Now I am not the best judge of distance, but this is not much of an exaggeration.

What was I to do? There I was, unarmed except for a twelve ounce Bud Light and too old and feeble to run in the house. I immediately thought of ol' Davy Crockett who "kilt a 'bar' when he was only three." Heck, I wasn't three, and I wasn't Davy Crockett. I was seventy-six years old, and I had nothing with which to defend myself except for one beer can in my hand. I sure was not going to throw it in any direction until it was emptied. I also suspected that the bear could run faster than me.

But all ended well, my friends. It is a common fact that many wild animals urinate to mark their territories and that is exactly what I did. I marked a circle around myself about three gallons wide, then for good measure, downed that twelve-ounce Bud Light and added a little more.

That ol' bear came charging on two legs, but suddenly halted just as it reached my marked territory. After sniffing a few times then eyeing me with a look of distain, off it went in another direction. My son who had been mowing three acres away finally arrived and I asked, "What took you so long?" He said, "There was nothing to worry about, dad. That bear is a female. She only drinks wine."

Old Folks Can Relate

On Getting Older

With another year having passed and the window narrowing on how many more are left, I have been doing a little reflection. I am now well into the eighth decade of my life. Before my generation, all the men in my family died before their sixtieth birthday. Well, I am seventy-six years old, apparently in decent health, and of fairly sound mind. That makes me sixteen years older than death, and I am still going strong. I have a loving wife, children and grandchildren, brother and sisters, and extended family with whom I maintain close contact. I am not in jail, and neither are any of my loved ones. We are all drug-free, have avoided poverty, and really enjoy our times together. No jealousies or family feuds to mar our relationships. Without a doubt, I have been truly blessed. So what now? Forgive me if I ramble a little bit, but I don't know any other way to express my feelings.

I fret about the little things. My wife shops too much–my opinion, not hers–and I can't convince her we are retired and on a fixed income. My children, although apparently successful and happy, are still a worry to me because they don't always do, think, or act the way I think they should. And the grandchildren, bless their hearts, didn't have the opportunity to be raised by me. If so, their grades would be better, their choices in music different, and their hair would be cut more often. Their eating habits would be healthier, and their choice of friends would be more to my liking. And they wouldn't leave my house a wreck when they visit.

I think about the future and wonder what happens next. I have a normal functioning mind now, but having watched loved ones suffer from dementia, I know things can change at any time. I feel good today, but so did Billy Sewell just a few days before he died. I cannot control the costs of future living and worry if I have enough to make it to the end...and while I don't dwell on it, I wonder how soon the end will come. I'm watching our country go down the wrong path and wonder why everyone else doesn't think or vote like me. I see the cost of health care spiraling upwards while knowing my own health will eventually start to go down. How in the heck am I going to afford to get sick? I have witnessed the death of good music as we once knew it. Whoever claimed that classic rock 'n' roll and traditional country were here to stay lied. I see political correctness replacing common sense and loyalty to political parties replacing loyalty to country. God has been kicked out of the schools, and they'll probably try to kick Him out of the churches next. Kids no longer know how to write and, with the proliferation of personal electronic devices, if they ever lose the use of their fingers, they will no longer be able to even talk to each other. And try reading one of their texts sometime. They evidently have also lost the ability to spell.

I am mentally young but trapped in an aging body that deceives other people into thinking I am a senile old codger. My muscular, suave, and quite attractive physique disappears whenever I step in front of a mirror. Those once quick reactions and keen eyesight are only fading memories. I run into dear friends on the street and usually recognize their faces but sometimes am very slow to recall their names. I don't really like to drive at night anymore and often fail to thank the good Lord that I still can drive at all. And I hate these new televisions and phones that are smarter than I am. The only drugs I've tried lately are all legal and prescribed by my doctors.

I could spend countless more hours rambling about the state of the life that I am leading. But why bother? Many reading this are about the same age as me and have their own problems and concerns. But our age has some benefits too. I can speak my mind and say anything I want to, and folks don't really take it personally. They blame it on old age. If some beautiful eighteen-year-old should entice me into her bedroom, I do not worry about getting her or me into trouble. That would require staying awake. If I get mad at someone, it is a sure thing I will get over it soon. That comes from not remembering that I was even mad. If I get stopped by a policeman, I am so naturally wobbly on my feet that they never think to give me a sobriety test. They usually ask if I need an ambulance. And if I want to put beer on my cornflakes for breakfast or use it for salad dressing at dinner, so what? At my age, the nourishment one gets from milk and salad dressing is overrated anyway.

Generally speaking, I have reached the age that, whenever I'm lucky enough to get myself into trouble I certainly don't regret it. I brag about it.

Enough of this. I got fifteen minutes older just writing these thoughts down. I've still got things to do and miles to go before I sleep and, hopefully, most of you will be a part of it. Life's adversities will need to step aside for a few more miles. There is still a lot of fun and interesting unknowns and maybe even a little trouble out there just waiting for ol' Jerry to show up. It might be getting late, but the party ain't over yet. I hope you all come along for the ride.

Television Questions for Those Over 70

Back in the late 1940s and almost entire decade of the 1950s, television was new, exciting, expanding, competing with radio, and finding its niche in the American home. Back then, for those of us lucky enough–and whose family was wealthy enough–to have a television in our homes, this wonderful new communication device bought much entertainment. Entire evenings and sometimes weekends were planned around what was showing at a particular time of day or evening. Reception was so spotty that we had to get out of our seats constantly to adjust the rabbit ears or go outside and turn the antenna in a different direction. Televisions were powered by vacuum tubes that were prone to frequent failure. Screens of the most expensive televisions were huge, or so we thought at the time, measuring up to 19 or 21 inches. All programs were shown in two colors, black and white. While viewing, the "snow" was occasionally so thick that we strained to see the image of what was actually showing on the screen. Fortunately, the sound was fairly constant with not too much static, even if it was being projected through a two or three-inch speaker. If we were lucky, we had our choice of three network channels or turn on the radio. Cable television was a dream that no one thought would become a reality. After all, who would actually pay for something they were already receiving for free?

As time passed and the media expanded, we evolved to where we are today: remote controls, hundreds of channels, thousands of programs, millions of commercials, around the clock coverage, wall-to-wall stereo surround sound, and pictures so clear that they make even the movie screens of our childhood pale by comparison. And all of this without rabbit ears or antennas to adjust. Some television screens are now almost as big as the movie screens of our childhood. We have family-friendly, PG, R-rated, NC-17, and unrated choices. We have networks dedicated to a single theme: e.g., news, opinion, movies, food, music, drama, cartoons, religion, etc. If we miss a favorite show, we can watch it a few hours later or the next day. There is no such thing as waiting for summer reruns. Of course, all this comes at a price.

Yeah, we have come a long way from those days of yore when daytime television consisted of game shows and soap operas while after-school programming included cartoons and Hopalong Cassidy. Local news was on at six and network news at six-thirty. Family shows were slated for the evening seven-to-nine o'clock timeslot. And all were shown at the same day and time of each week. If a program had a "damn" or "hell" uttered, it either aired after nine o'clock or was banned outright. We never got to see anything with overtly sexual content. Graphic violence, while sometimes implied, was never shown. Late news was always at eleven o'clock on all three channels and sign off was at eleven-thirty or midnight. Saturdays would bring a single "baseball game of the week" and, on good weekends, two channels might carry football games. And they were kind enough to not air them at the same time. And maybe, on Saturday night, one of the channels would remain on after the late news and show an old movie. And no matter what day it was, for those who got up too early in the morning or stayed up too late at night, there was always a test pattern to watch.

Yes, the times and technology have certainly changed. The electronics are fantastic. The availability, quality, clarity, and choice of programs are overwhelming. But has it all been for the better?

So finally, here is my question: do you enjoy television more today that you did a few generations ago?

Sadness in Tennessee

February 27, 2016: Today my heart is saddened, and there is a tear in my eye. The University of Tennessee meant well when they sent me their Spring/Summer 2016 Non-Credit Course Catalog this week. They broke my heart instead. I want to say "darn you," but it is not their fault. In fact, they are trying to do the right thing with their latest course offering. But the fact they even feel obligated to offer the course is disheartening.

I know that technology changes. We have gone from vinyl records to eight-track tapes to cassette tapes to CDs to iPods to who knows what, and the music has survived. Computer processing has gone from a house-sized machine to a room-sized machine to a desktop to a tablet to a processor the size of a pack of cigarettes or smaller with huge increases in the computing power and nothing lost in the transition. But this time it is different. This time it is personal.

Here is what has me so upset. I quote from page 16 of the University of Tennessee catalog mentioned above:

> **Cursive Handwriting**
> **(Grades 3–6, rising)**
> **If you've never been taught to read or write in cursive,**

fear not—you are not alone! Unfortunately, many kids have missed the opportunity to learn cursive and cannot sign their own names. But with the help of this interactive, hands-on camp, you'll learn how to write in cursive legibly as well as how to read cursive in letters and historical documents. Once you get the hang of it, you'll even have the opportunity to learn and practice the beautiful style of calligraphy. Instructor: Laura Arnette Smith

Course # 16SU344 Fee: $129

Mon-Fri, 6/13/2016-6/17/2016, 1:15 PM to 4:15 PM, 5 classes

UT Conference Center, downtown Knoxville

Reread the description of this course. "*Many kids...cannot sign their own names*" and "*you'll learn how to...read...letters and historical documents.*" What a rude awakening to the state of our current education system. But why should I be so upset? After all, why do kids need to know cursive plus how to print? Isn't one method enough for successful communication? Some would argue that teaching the current generation two methods of writing is just a waste of time. They have a point.

I would argue that since the day of our founding fathers and well before then, cursive writing was the primary vehicle for recording the great and small events of the times. It was the method for relaying thought and ideas of a business, personal, and scientific nature. It was a way for loved ones to communicate when apart. Sure, many of the ideas and communications once recorded in cursive are now captured within the various modern electronic devices which we use. But many are not. No computer carries the correspondence of my great-grandfather or grandfather. No computer carries the beloved recipes of my grandmother or mother. No electronic device contains the letters written between two lovers who were members of my family and a part of my heritage. And as my grandchildren or their children lose the ability to read the English language as written in cursive, many pieces of our history will be lost forever.

Yes, I am old and set in my ways. Yes, I am stubborn and sometimes refuse to change. Yes, I am mad that cursive is no longer being taught in many of our schools. Yes, I am sad and heartbroken that a way of life is going the way of other obsolete communications such as Latin and the Cherokee alphabet. Yes, I am glad, I guess, that the University of Tennessee is trying in their small way to correct a wrong by offering this course.

But I ask you, and forgive my language, how in Hades are they going to teach their target audience to read, write, and interpret cursive writing in five days? I must have been a slow learner while growing up because it took me years to master the art. And I will do everything I can to see that the art isn't lost by or denied to my children, grandchildren, and those that follow.

And finally, ask yourself if there is some sort of conspiracy going on: why are all our newspapers, books, electronic devices, and systems, etc., designed to depict all writing in print form instead of cursive? Here we are in the middle of the space generation, and there is almost no one left with the *write* stuff.

How Stupid Can One Be?

Forgive me for cluttering up your thought process again, but I must ask, how stupid can one be? Let me explain.

Sharon has been trying to get me to convert to a smartphone for a couple of years now. I am old, set in my ways, and I unashamedly cling to the past. I never wanted to own any electronic device smarter than me. I have refused to give in to her constant nagging about this matter. Then she goes and steals the old television out of the den and moves it to "her" room. Well, what is a guy to do? Basketball season is ongoing, golf is underway, and the new football season will be here in a few months. When it comes to men and watching sports on their televisions, nothing but the biggest, best, and finest will do. Yeah, how stupid can one be?

I purchased a new television last week, and now I don't know what to do with it. It looks nice, has a 65-inch screen, is supposed to be top of the line, and might even work. I may never know. For you see, I screwed up and brought a smart television. In fact, it might be ultra-smart. No, it goes further than that. It might even be a genius. One thing is for sure, my 170 or perhaps slightly less IQ is no match for it. In fact, this thing is so impressive that I mortgaged the house to help pay for it. How stupid can one be?

So I get the new television home and quickly unpack it, set it on the television stand, and plug it in. I called my good friend David King and, between the two of us, we had no problem at all loading the batteries in the remote. But when I turned the television on for the first time, all hell broke loose. The television came alive but in a most ugly way. It wanted my email address, password, and life history just to identify that I was the rightful owner. Then it asked for my Wi-Fi password, the name of my first wife and her current boyfriend, and what kind of beer I had in the refrigerator. I evidently answered all of the questions correctly because it then told me that I was now authorized to proceed to the next step. I agreed to do so. How stupid can one be?

The next step was to simply refer to the instruction manual for final setup. I did so. The printed manual packed in the box was three pages long. Two and three-quarters pages were warnings to not spill water or pee on the television while it was plugged in. Finally, the last sentence said to use the remote to access the e-manual for further instructions. So, like an idiot, I picked up the remote with all the confidence in the world that I could accomplish this simple task. How stupid can one be?

I have never seen a remote like this one. It is six inches long by one and three-eighths inches wide. It has no number buttons (0 thru 9), nothing labeled as Power, Mute, Source, Tools, Return, Info, Exit, Last Channel, Menu, Favorite Channel, etc. It had three unlabeled buttons but none that had arrows indicating Up, Down, Left, or Right. The only written words on it are Vol, Ch, and Samsung. Nothing told me how to get to the e-manual, and I have pushed every button in every possible manner with both the left and right hands, using every finger in every possible combination without success. None of the toes on my left or right feet work either. How stupid can one be?

Being the kind of man that I am, I refuse to ask for help or directions, so please don't respond to this little tale of woe. I am one of those lucky guys that have both a nine-year-old and a ten-year-old grandson. I can't wait until spring break when they can come to visit and get my television working in short order. And I have plenty of time to decide how to answer when they get around to asking, "Granddad, how stupid can one be?"

In the meantime, I will just enjoy reading a few good books. Real ones, of course; I'll not be using a Kindle.

Vacation Confusion

I cannot fault the Canadians for their use of the metric system, for they are in step with most of the world. I cannot fault the United States for clinging to the old English system of measurement, for that is all we've known since our birth as a nation. And I cannot blame our U.S. education system for my translation inadequacies for, best as I can remember, they tried to teach me the difference between the two different units of measurement. And really, who cares?

I didn't...but then I did.

Then there is the issue of money. Both countries speak the same language relative to currency. We mutually understand the concept of pennies, nickels, dimes, quarters, half dollars, and dollars. But there is one problem. It is called an exchange rate. All dollars are not equal. And to confuse things further, the exchange rate changes daily. And really, who cares?

I didn't...but then I did.

Sharon and I just spent eight days in Canada. We crossed the border at Detroit and drove into Windsor, Canada. Suddenly the road signs quit telling us how many miles we were from our destination. They were now telling us the distance in kilometers. Also, the speed limit was now posted in kilometers per hour instead of miles per hour. As we drove out of town toward Toronto on this nice superhighway the road sign indicated the speed limit was 100 kilometers per hour. Well, I immediately sped up and was doing only 95 miles per hour when I passed the cop. Sharon gently reminded me the KM to MPH conversion was not one-to-one and I might be traveling a little above the speed limit. My Oak Ridge education belatedly kicked in, and I recalled that 100 kilometers per hour converts to a speed of approximately 62 miles per hour. I suspected the cop would agree with my calculations, so I sped up until I lost him.

Fortunately, my Honda Ridgeline was smarter than me, and all I had to do was push a button to convert my speedometer to kilometers per hour. I did not speed after that, but I still struggled to convert kilometers to miles relative to how far away we were from our destination. When you see a road sign that says you are 132 kilometers from Bobcaygeon, Ontario, how far are you really away? My mind went into calculator mode for the rest of the trip.

Then I stopped for gas. In Oak Ridge, I am used to seeing the big neon sign at the gas station showing something like $2.09 per gallon. The first gas station sign I saw in Canada indicated $1.01.9. Heck, I was ready to jump on that! It was only after I filled up and paid $68.00 Canadian that I realized that the gas was priced per liter rather than per gallon. Then I had to mentally calculate a liter to gallon conversion. Again, thanks to my Oak Ridge education, I finally figured out that a liter was 0.26 of a gallon. This meant that I was paying around four bucks per gallon rather than the bargain I first thought I was getting. But as upset as I was at the price, I forgot all about the conversion rate of the American to Canadian Dollar, which helped ease the pain a little.

During our trip, the American dollar was worth about twenty to twenty-eight cents more than the Canadian dollar. So while everything we purchased in Canada seemed more expensive than in the U.S., I would have to mentally subtract twenty to twenty-five percent from the advertised Canadian price to understand my true cost. Sharon did not have this problem. She bought everything she wanted and let me worry about the conversion rates. I suspect I will be filing for bankruptcy when the American Express and Visa bills arrive.

The other odd thing about Canadian money is they have no one-cent pieces nor paper currency for the equivalent of our one and two-dollar bills. All cash exchanges that end in an odd amount are rounded up or down to the nearest nickel. And instead of having paper one and two-dollar bills, they have coins. The dollar coin is called a "Loonie," and the two-dollar coin is called the "Toonie." And that sums up our trip. We felt like we were in an old Saturday matinee showing of a Loony-Toons cartoon at the Center Theatre in Jackson Square. But we had a great time anyway and came home broke as usual. Anybody hiring?

And if you've been bored by my narrative, it could have been worse. I could have shown you our vacation pictures instead.

Bad News for Old Folks

Today I discovered that most of us born in the early 1940s or earlier are dead. This is based on science and statistics, not hearsay, so do not try to convince me otherwise. In the year most of my high school classmates were born, the average life expectancy for men was around 62 years and 68 years for women. By the time we reached our senior year in high school, the average life expectancy was increased to around 67 years for men and 73 years for women. But keep in mind, this increase was based on those folks being born in 1959, not those born in the early 40s. I know we have lost some beloved classmates and other friends our age in the past, so science was probably right about them. But what about the rest of us? We are well past our projected life expectancy. Our time has expired but, evidently, we somehow have not realized it nor given in to it. Folks, we are now in scary territory. We are either way above average or already dead and do not know it. So, what is next?

As you know, weekends are for parties, and we have a weekend coming up. Don't take this personal, but I am calling it the Weekend of the Living Dead. What that means is, no matter where the gathering is at, you need to show up, and party like there is no tomorrow! See you there.

Poems

Dreaming

If I had one dream to wish come true,
Without hesitation I'd dream of you...
I'd take you away to a world of my own
Where, for a time, you'd be mine alone.
I'd give you much pleasure while we were there;
Pleasing and teasing, and showing I care.
I would hold you so close to allay the great fear
That my dream wasn't real and you'd soon disappear.
With a heartbeat like thunder and a soul full of yearning
I'd caress you and kiss you while the bridges were burning.
And gently we'd love, with thoughts warm and tender,
Creating a moment to forever remember.
Then when our time passed and reality did call,
We'd return so quietly as tho' we weren't gone at all;
There'd be no regrets, nor pondering our fate;
No shattered emotions to turn into hate;
Just a personal feeling between me and you...
If dreams came true.

The Clowns

She laughs, she cries, she brightens his day.
She is faithful and true and always a friend.
She warms his heart in a most special way,
A relationship he prays that will endure without end.
She sees but one facet, 'tis surface he shows,
Masking emotions and feelings locked safely away.
The nonchalance of his face hides the pain that he knows,
The clown keeps smiling and continues to play.
He is near yet so far, he can be touched not at all.
Inside a clown's heart there will never be peace,
She waits so patiently for him merely to call,
While inside her soul the tears will not cease.
He laughs, he cries, he brightens her day,
He is faithful and true and always a friend;
His charm warms her heart in a most special way,
Yet, she cracks not the door to let him come in.
They remain only friends, too afraid or unsure
To open their hearts, not even a fraction.
Those glowing embers of passion so intense and so pure
Are quenched by the fear each has of the other's reaction.
Thus through the irony of fate two clown's lives touch,
Both carrying emotions the other can't see.
Because of false fears they will never love too much...

Can this perhaps be the story of you and me?

On Being Alone

Lonely am I in the dark of the night;
I hear my tears fall with a sound that is quiet.
  That bottle of gin
  Is my only friend;
The silence is deafening, the dark is too bright.
The morning awakes but I cannot stir;
For my head keeps spinning, a demon lurks there.
  Windows are doors,
  Ceilings are floors,
And strange, weird monsters fly through the air.
Did I fall asleep or am I dead?
No, death is better than this pain in my head.
  This is no tomb,
  It is a room,
And there is my bottle, lying on the bed.
Slowly, painfully, I arise to my feet,
Wondering if the strain will stop my heartbeat.
  But, on the bed
  The bottle is dead;
I collapse to the floor and face final defeat.

Thinking of You

Although I'm with you on occasion
I want you every day;
To hold and kiss and touch and love
In each and every way.
Just one word or look from you
Can fill me with desire.
You're like a flame that is burning bright
And I am drawn to fire.
I'll do my best to make you happy
As long as I am near
And pray the day will never come
When I must disappear.
If, someday, you read my thoughts,
You'll know these words are true;
Not because you're just anyone
But, because you're you.

Thirty-Nine and Counting

As time marches on, so do our fears
If we worry about it and count all the years...

Our blood pressure rises, our aches become pain;
We may have trouble remembering our name.
Our hopes become memories and we start to pray
That our eyesight won't dim and our hair won't turn gray.
For some people tho', there's no denying their fate.
Why worry about gray hair when it's already too late?
We still think and feel young–we refuse to quit
but acknowledge at times that we've slowed down a bit.
We look in the mirror and are more thick than thin
And spot a new wrinkle where there once was smooth skin.
As we fight off senility, for the old days we yearn;
At least back then we still had bridges to burn.

The point to be made while our troubles are mounting
Is "Don't give a darn, why bother with counting."

A Proposal

I love you with the deepness of depth, and the joy of desire;
And with a longing within me which my soul cannot bear.
I need you beside me to travel the long road
While the aura of your nearness helps lighten my load.
Through the dark and the light; through both heaven and hell,
Your sweet, tender voice can make everything well.
Like a bird on the wing or the flight of a dove,
My burdens will be lifted by the touch of your love.
Please love me, my darling, belong only to me;
"Till death do us part" our love shall be.

Tribute (?) To The Girls of the Class of 59

Popular or boring, outgoing or shy,
Fat, thin, tall, or small;
The Oak Ridge women, Class of '59,
Made no difference, I loved them all.
Ballgames, bowling, movies and more;
Yes, it was a magical time back then;
Joys and heartaches and memories galore,
You became acquaintance, wife, lover, and friend.
But face it ladies, almost sixty years have passed,
Things have changed, 'tis true.
Until this reunion I had oft times wondered...
What the heck happened to you?
Well, now I know.
Your hair has been doctored but I've spotted much gray
And you've picked up a pound or two
You walk down the street and nobody whistles,
But that is what Age will do.
Oh, you still look good, girl, but it takes much longer
To repair that elderly face;
Makeup retards the march of time
But your wrinkles are winning the race.
You go to the doctor more often now
And have been subjected to numerous tests.
How long, I wonder, until you concede
There's no cure for sagging breasts.
But our good doctors can help you yet,
They've made some tremendous gains
In surgical removal of another concern

Some of the Girls of the Class of 1959

Known medically as varicose veins.
The fanny droops, and it's time for false teeth;
Yes, that is what aging will cause.
For those of sound mind just try to remember
Life before menopause.
And when it comes to your mind
It is hard to speak out;
There is just so darned little
To talk about.
And as for your sex life, ladies,
I bet you're not as resistant.
Funny how one's attitude changes
When it's nearly nonexistent.
Removing Depends rather than sexy panties
Does "dampen" the urge to play.

But to that man of yours it makes no difference;
If he can't get it up anyway.
I could continue but it's time to shut up
And for those who now wish me dead,
I'm not worried for before you take action
You'll forget just what I've said.
So, to you girls who have good memories,
Most of what I've said is true;
Please be aware this was aimed at a classmate
I would never direct this at you.
Popular or boring, outgoing or shy,
Fat, thin, tall, or small:
The Oak Ridge women, Class of '59 –
The greatest ever and I'll *always* love you all!

Ode to Aging

A few days ago my birthday came then went away.
It left me a lot more bald and a little more gray.
I now move some slower or not at all.
My bones are shrinking and I'm not as tall.
The aches and pains, they make me groan
And I'm less upright and a lot more prone.
But, when I'm able, I still stand tall;
The pills work well when I remember to take them all.
I went to meet some of my friends but they didn't look right...
Is it them or just my bad eyesight?
I drove to the bar and I really must say,
More and more drivers had to get out of my way.
They were wrong when they cursed.
After all, I was driving on their side first.
Then at the bar, those gals were sleazy;
Made a big move, thought I was easy.
They didn't realize Sharon was my current and not my ex.
Those girls were interested only in sex.
Maybe when I get a little older and start to tremble
I won't be such a desirable sex symbol.
Little did they know, these ol' girlfriends,
That I had traded in my Speedos for size large Depends.
But all in all, I cannot complain
Except for not being able to remember my name.
So I just drink my beer on which I thrive;
It's great celebrating just being alive.

Amen.

A Birthday Toast to a Far Away Friend

Birthdays come and birthdays go;
some too fast and some too slow.
Some are fun and some are sad,
They're sometimes good and sometimes bad.
Some are special and some are not;
Some are remembered and some forgot.
Some friends visit or maybe phone
While others leave you all alone.
Some parties are big and some are small.
And some are given not at all.
Some love you daily and call you dear;
Others just call maybe once a year.
Some look and think, "I just want to hold her."
Others may think, "She's looking older."
But special friends do special things,
Sometimes more thoughtful than diamond rings.
They write dumb things that sometimes rhyme.
Some are so bad it's almost a crime.
But some are most meaningful and set apart.
They come not from the mind but from the heart.
So like it or not, I tell you true,
This one is my favorite for it is written for you.
May your birthday bash be the best one yet...
And by the way, before I forget...
This toast to you makes me sad, tis' true:

Sure wish I was there to share it with you.

Ode to the Ladies in Blue–Season I

From out of the ashes of a prime long past,
Arose a team destined to finish last.
Their grit and determination is a matter of fact;
They did all that was necessary to keep their record intact.
They were deterred not at all by any lack of real skill,
And knew from the first practice that it would all be uphill.
So with bonds of real friendship and a spirit de corps;
They suffered great pain and begged the coaches for more.
Whether hitting or fielding or throwing the ball,
Their skills were all equal and not good at all.
And the speed on the base paths caused quite a commotion;
It was like watching a playback in extra slow motion.
With more agony than ecstasy they rounded into shape,
Then added a few pounds from the hops and the grape.
Looking like warriors but with thoughts like dumb cattle;
They fatefully, foolishly, claimed they were ready for battle.

So they hitched up their jockstraps and picked up their balls,
Bats, glove, and make-up, and who knows what all.
But all the joking and laughter was suddenly cut still;
By a team of gorillas upon Pinewood Field.
Well there was mayhem and slaughter that took place that day,
It was obvious from the beginning that only one team could play.
But God, with great mercy, did finally arrive;
And helped the ladies in blue to just barely survive.
The season thus started as the season did end,
With many a fight but nary a win.

But in truthfulness, I'll say, without too much boasting-
"You girls were all winners but suffered bad coaching!"
So let's party tonight then look forward to next year,
When you'll whip those teams that the bravest men fear.
As you get more aggressive and stronger and bolder;
Try to remember to forget that you'll be another year older.

Ode to the Ladies in Blue–Season II

This summer there were some softball games
Played at Robertsville
By a group of women who thought real young
But moved like over-the-hill.
They were mentally quick but physically slow
And never the twain did meet;
The ravages of time had taken its toil
So never a team was beat.
They showed up sober, they showed up drunk,
They showed up weak and lame;
And like good Christians all prayed together,
"Dear Lord, please let it rain."
Well, rain it did, each and every game,
It seemed almost like a vision;
But instead of water falling on the ground
It was base hits by the opposition.
Don't fault our fielders of great confidence
Displayed for all to see.
They yelled to the batter before each pitch.
"Please don't hit it at me."
At each big swing they'd quickly react;
I've seen no greater play;
The diving, the twisting, the jumping and running
To get out of the way.
Now, Blue's time to bat, the tables were turned;
No fear in their faces at all.
With dreams of home runs and bodies of sweat
They stepped up to hit the ball.

The first two pitches were of little concern
Yet they soon began to pout
When the umpire's arm went up in the air
And he said, "Strike three, you're out."
And so it went, game after game,
The ump kept making those sounds.
The biggest reason they could not hit
Was from carrying the extra pounds.
It is tough to win or even get close,
At least so thought their mates,
When playing teams who are lean and mean
While being heavyweights.
Yet let's give credit where credit is due;
They tried and tried some more,
Not to win, that was an impossible dream,
But just to make a score.
In a game or two they did score a run
So to them I raise my cup.
You can shut them out just so many times
But never shut them up.
The only way to sum up the year
Is to turn time back a day
And hear the words of Grantland Rice,
Here is what he had to say:
"When the Great Scorekeeper comes to write against your name,
He writes not whether you won or lost but how you played the game."
Contemplate these words of wisdom,
Interpret them as you will,

While I leave you with just one last thought
Of how I personally feel:
Mr. Rice's composition is deeply profound,
With words he had a way;
But I wonder aloud, would he have written those words
If he had ever seen them play?

On Contemplating My Own Mortality

That train of life just keeps going faster
And time I am starting to lack;
Ahead, somewhere, more sooner than later,
There awaits the end of the track.

Now I've lived fast and I've lived reckless,
Never needed to look around;
The dreams I sought were there for the taking,
Then life upped and knocked me down.

They shot that dye up through my heart,
The ol' doc just shook his head;
"Jerry, I don't know why you are alive and kicking.
Most folks would now be dead."

With the stroke of a scalpel my chest lay open,
The beat of life was thin;
Then four bypasses and a few hours later
They sewed me up again.

I came back fully in no time at all,
Hard times, they couldn't last.
The past was past, the healing complete...
Then the skies turned overcast.
Adversity struck and hit me hard
Though I'm doing good so far,
After they left me with a lot less cancer
And twelve more inches of scar.

So it was back to work and back to play,
I've avoided that final call.
But a nagging thought still lingers near:
I wonder if they got it all?
And there's been an illness here, an injury there
As the years keep passing by;
But between the lows there's been much joy
So I laugh instead of cry.

The ol' grim reaper, he's cracked a smile
But I'll tell you one thing my friend;
When counting me out he's twice reached seven
But he darned sure hasn't reached ten.

Of course the time will come, I hope its later,
That I'll again have to face strike three,
And whether I'm out or foul it off
Will depend on more than me.

The Good Lord likes me, I'm not sure why,
So whatever trial I'll face,
I'll have a chance, not because I deserve it
But through His loving grace.

So when my time on earth is finally over,
Shed no sad tears for me.
Just raise your glass in that bar not passed
And drink to my memory.
But before I go, a final request

As you add another year;
If you'll buy me a beer for your birthday
I can drink it while I'm still here!

Acknowledgments

Little did I know what I was getting into when I decided to compile my various writings into a book. I would not have survived the ordeal without the help of some people who are smarter than me.

Thank you to a wonderful group of friends that I call the '59 Chatters. This is a small group of special folks with whom I graduated from Oak Ridge High School in 1959 and maintain close contact today. They know who they are so I will not name them here. Without even realizing it, they provided much inspiration, motivation, encouragement and even criticism to help me compose many of the stories.

John Haffey and Jim McKay were particularly helpful in reviewing, critiquing, and editing the various drafts that I struggled with during the many days putting the final product together. Thanks, John and Jim, you both are real winners. If Sharon increases my allowance like she promised, I will buy you both a beer.

A special place in my heart is reserved for Sandra Whitten Plant: journalist, author, instructor, editor, and dear friend. Her suggestions, guidance, editorial skills, and experience were invaluable, and she sent me back to the drawing board more than once because she knew I could do better than the draft she was reading. The drinks are on me, girl. You've earned them.

And finally, what can I say about my dear wife, Sharon? She not only unwittingly provided much raw material for my writings but also tolerated my poking fun in her direction too many times. Also, I am an old codger whose computer skills are almost nonexistent. Without her Information Technology support, this publication would not exist. I think I will keep her around another fifty-three years. Thanks also to my two sons, Kevin and Andrew. The ol' man appreciates the two of you and does not tell you that often enough.

And, of course, Two Peas Publishing was there when I needed them. If mistakes or errors were found in my writings, do not blame them. They are not responsible for the contents but are surely responsible for improving what they had to work with. They made an old man look better than he deserved.

About the Author

Jerry L. Harris provided a summary of his adult life in the *Family* section of this book in an article titled *About My Wife and Me*. What he failed to provide was that he spent his childhood years in Bluefield, Virginia, then moved to Oak Ridge, Tennessee, when he was in the seventh grade. He graduated from Oak Ridge High School in 1959 then attended both the University of Tennessee and East Tennessee State University. After college, he worked briefly for the Federal Housing Administration in Washington, D.C.

In 1962, President Lyndon B. Johnson sent Mr. Harris a personal letter inviting him to report to the Clinton, Tennessee, bus station where he would be transported to Knoxville, Tennessee, for induction into the U.S. Army. Mr. Harris showed up and spent two years serving his country, mostly with the Army's 12th Artillery Group located at Oklahoma City Air Force Station, Oklahoma City, Oklahoma.

After being honorably discharged from the service, Mr. Harris spent the next forty-one years and fourteen days employed at the Department of Energy's facilities in Oak Ridge. For most of those years, he worked at the Y-12 National Security Complex.

Jerry is not a professional writer but honed his skills writing quality assurance procedures, technical manuals, position papers, etc., for the vast bureaucracy of the federal government. He also humored friends and coworkers with occasional *ad hoc* papers and stories about life behind the security fences. After retirement in 2007, he has done nothing really worthwhile with his life but does putter around on the computer composing tales for his friends scattered around the country.

Sweeping Out the Attic is Mr. Harris's first book, and he claims his mind is now empty and he will probably not publish another one. Jerry and his wife, Sharon, continue to live in Oak Ridge, Tennessee. They have two sons, two daughters-in-law and four grandsons.

The author does not have a website, but he can be contacted via email at harrisjl1@outlook.com.

The author and his wife,
Jerry and Sharon Harris

the End

CPSIA information can be obtained
at www.ICGtesting.com
Printed in the USA
LVHW03s0724200818
587459LV00002B/2/P

9 781938 271410